EMPATH & PSYCHIC ABILITIES

YOUR PRACTICAL GUIDE TO EASING OVERWHELM, PROTECTING YOUR ENERGY, GAINING CONFIDENCE IN YOUR GIFTS & DEVELOPING YOUR INTUITIVE ABILITIES TO UNLOCK YOUR SIXTH SENSE

THEMAGICWITHIN

Copyright © 2023 TheMagicWithin. All rights reserved.

The content within this book may not be reproduced, duplicated, or transmitted without direct written permission from the author or the publisher.

Under no circumstances will any blame or legal responsibility be held against the publisher, or author, for any damages, reparation, or monetary loss due to the information contained within this book, either directly or indirectly.

Legal Notice:

This book is copyright protected. It is only for personal use. You cannot amend, distribute, sell, use, quote, or paraphrase any part of the content within this book, without the consent of the author or publisher.

Disclaimer Notice:

Please note the information contained within this document is for educational and entertainment purposes only. All effort has been expended to present accurate, up-to-date, reliable, and complete information. No warranties of any kind are declared or implied. Readers acknowledge that the author is not engaged in the rendering of legal, financial, medical, or professional advice. The content within this book has been derived from various sources. Please consult a licensed professional before attempting any techniques outlined in this book.

By reading this document, the reader agrees that under no circumstances is the author responsible for any losses, direct or indirect, that are incurred as a result of the use of the information contained within this document, including, but not limited to, errors, omissions, or inaccuracies.

CONTENTS

About the Author & Introduction — 9
What To Expect From This Guide — 13

Part I
UNDERSTANDING YOUR EMPATH GIFTS

Part I Chapter 1 — 19
What is an Empath & Are You One?

Part I Chapter 2 — 27
The Science Behind Being An Empath

Part II
PROTECTING YOUR PRECIOUS ENERGY

Part II Chapter 1 — 35
Energy Vampires, Negative Nancies and Other Nasties (and how to protect yourself from them)

Part II Chapter 2 — 45
Picking The Right People

Part II Chapter 3 — 53
Call in Backup!

Part II Chapter 4 — 59
Furry Friends and The Crazy Bird Lady

Part II Chapter 5 — 63
Environment

Part III
EMBRACING YOUR EMPATH TRAITS AND OVERCOMING OVERWHELM

Part III Chapter 1 — 71
Embracing Sensitivity and Alone Time

Part III Chapter 2 — 81
Finding An Outlet For Your Rollercoaster Of Emotions

Part III Chapter 3 — 87
Use Your Gifts To Help Others

Part IV
UNLOCKING YOUR SIXTH SENSE AND DISCOVERING YOUR PSYCHIC ABILITIES

Part IV Chapter 1 — 99
Introduction To Your Sixth Sense And Psychic Abilities

Part IV Chapter 2 — 105
Deepening Your Psychic Abilities

Part IV Chapter 3 — 113
Developing Your Empath Abilities Into Mediumship

Part IV Chapter 4 — 121
Connecting With Your Guides

Part IV Chapter 5 — 131
Clairvoyance Abilities

Part IV Chapter 6 — 141
The Power & Purpose Of Dreams

Part IV Chapter 7 — 151
Psychic Attacks and Protection

Part V
USING YOUR EMPATH POWERS TO WORK WITH THE UNIVERSE

Part V Chapter 1 — 165
Manifestation & Working With The Universe

Part V Chapter 2 — 175
Crystals

Conclusion — 183
References — 189

WELCOME!

Samaria here, founder of TheMagicWithin. Before we start on this journey together, I want to give you a present because I'm a giver, just like you!

At TheMagicWithin our aim is to help women discover their inner magic to gain confidence and clarity.
One of the best ways to do this is through meditation.
*So just email the word '**Meditation**' to **samaria@themagicwithin.world** to gain access to some free meditations that I know can help any empath on their journey.*

Join TheMagicWithin Family!

If you'd like to connect with a community of like-minded, caring souls, come and join our MagicWithin family on social media!

*You can find us on **Instagram at @TheMagicWithin_**
Or come and hang out in our **private Facebook group:**
TheMagicWithin*

*And if you'd like more regular tips on everything from harnessing your empath traits & sensitivity, to improving confidence and clarity in all areas of your life, send us an email here to join our email list: **samaria@themagicwithin.world** (we won't send you a load of spammy rubbish, promise!)*

DISCLAIMER

The guidance in this book isn't intended to replace any medical treatment plans prescribed by a doctor or other medical professional. If you're suffering with mental or physical health issues please consult a qualified healthcare professional as well as exploring holistic options. TheMagicWithin and the author of this book will not be liable for any outcome of not seeking proper medical advice where needed.

ABOUT THE AUTHOR & INTRODUCTION

'I realised one night in LA that the purpose of my life had always been to free people from concern.' The only one I hadn't freed was myself'

~ Jim Carrey

I had a similar realisation about 10 years ago after another night of tossing and turning in my bed. Suffocated by an overwhelming sense of emotional heaviness, I'd spent the day absorbing the energies of those around me. I was drained, overwhelmed and over it.

I had no idea at the time that such a thing as an *'Empath'* existed. I had no idea that I was one. I just knew I felt.. *different.*

Overwhelm was the norm, paired with a side of high sensitivity, a deep desire to be alone, and an extra helping of easily triggered overstimulation, I didn't realise that life didn't feel quite so stirring for most people.

Though I often romanticised it, I just thought life was heavy, for everyone. But I thought that if I could somehow fix everyone's problems that always seemed to attach themselves to me, things would get lighter.

Moving into my teenage years some of my friends called me a people pleaser, which annoyed me because it was true. And for a long time I continued on my mission of innocent but soul sucking people pleasing in an attempt to brighten the world of those around me. In some ways I succeeded, but there wasn't much light or energy left for myself at times, *sound familiar?*

It wasn't all gloomy though. I also often felt elated at times, especially when people around me felt that way, or when there was a nice sunset, moving music, or cancelled social plans *(that was the ultimate win!)*.

But what was this up, down, light and dark all about?

At 19 years old the answer hit me like a brick. Well, it hit me more like a sprinkling of comfort and reassurance really, because I stumbled upon *'The Happy Empath'* by Christine Rose Elle, and her description of an empath resonated with me to the core of my being.

Reading someone's words that described my coping mechanisms that I hadn't, until that moment, realised were coping mechanisms, showed me that I wasn't alone in feeling like the world could be heavy. I wasn't the only one who had a habit of picking up and holding onto other peoples feelings as if I'd just found a rare $50 bill on the floor. I wasn't the only one who felt like I needed a long rest in a dark room after every social interaction, and I wasn't the only one who felt highly emotional and sensitive, with a strong passionate urge to help others but who often forgot to care for themself. This author prompted my research into empaths and I realised that all of these things I'd been experiencing were typical traits. This gave me a pivotal sense of relief.

Us humans have this common desire to want to categorise ourselves or diagnose our traits as conditions for comfort. At this point I really wasn't looking to do that, but for the first time I understood why we do it; it was seriously reassuring to put a name to my experiences, and to know that there were others just like me out there. Maybe you're not sure if you're an empath yet, in which case I hope this book brings you the clarity and reassurance you might be seeking. Because for me, learning that other people had figured out how to work with their empath traits rather than being weighed down by them, was the most comfort I'd probably ever felt. It meant that I wasn't weird or too sensitive or too different, or that I should just live with the heaviness forever. I was gifted, I wasn't alone and I had feasible solutions available to help me with the not-so-nice side of being an empath. This gave me hope.

And my hope for you is that this book offers even just a small sweet slice of the comfort that I felt when I picked up The Happy Empath at 19. My even stronger desire is that as you navigate through your own journey, you come to see your empath traits as true gifts - because that is what I finally know them to be.

As you've picked up this book, I'm guessing you're not quite there yet. You might be used to wondering if you're just a little crazy, maybe even mentally unhinged or just *'too sensitive'*, because of how you cope and react in daily life. Maybe those you know have tried to convince you of these possibilities, and while every option should of course be explored, I'd love you to explore the possibility of being none of those things. Because maybe those labels have been placed on you due to the limited consciousness and understanding of those you know. Maybe it's easier to accept the default *'crazy'* or *'different'* labels because those are much more commonly accepted over being an *'Empath'*. Maybe, if you can accept yourself and your gifts as being greater than what others try to label you as, then you'll realise the true infinite power that you hold. A level of power that will see your intuition stronger, your confidence skyrocket, and your overwhelm lose its hold.

Since harnessing my gifts I've experienced huge positive shifts in my life and I have no doubt that you can do the same. I've gone from being weighed down by heavy energy and emotions, unaware of my true inner power and potential, to living a life of pleasure, peace and fulfilment, all thanks to the mental shifts and techniques you're about to be provided with.

As a coach, creative and proud empath, nothing makes me happier than helping someone just like the younger me on their journey. So thank you for picking up this book and trusting me with your time and precious energy, and thank you for being the open and magical person that you are *(we'll be exploring that magic very soon)*.

It's time to tap into your gifts and enter a world beyond the mundane and physical. I welcome you lovingly on this journey and I thank you in advance for sharing your gifts with the world - it's time to harness them as you discover your inner magic.

Samaria x
~ TheMagicWithin

WHAT TO EXPECT FROM THIS GUIDE

Being an empath is a bit of a rollercoaster ride. You start out thinking, *"oh, this is cool, I'm totally in tune with the world around me"*, and then bam, the roiling emotions come a-knocking. Heart palpitating, ears ringing, and a light sweat beading on your brow, you suddenly realise all that comes with being an empath. But thankfully it's not as scary as it sounds *(or might feel!)*. It's actually a sweet gift, even if a little sickening at times.

Maybe you're not quite sure if you even are an empath yet, in which case this book can help you to decide. Whatever your verdict, if you're someone with high sensitivity, carrying chaotic or overwhelming energy, and possess a seemingly unshakable habit of breaking your boundaries for others, you'll benefit regardless from the journey you're about to embark on. This guide is here to steer you in a more peaceful direction and show you ways of dealing with the emotions and effects that come with being an empath, as well as helping you to discover all the benefits of possessing this superpower.

You're about to set off on a journey of boundary setting, emotional regulation and energy protection practices to keep the negativity away and your spirit strong. From overwhelmed and full of internal chaos, to ready to face the world with unshakable peace and power, you have an exciting ride ahead of you.

And that's not all..

There's a lot more to being an empath than meets the eye. *We're pretty magical actually!*

Our deep intuition and openness makes us more susceptible to experiences and connections that the typical person may never even comprehend. So in this book you'll also be exploring how to use your intuition to harness a whole range of talents that you may not know you have. From enhancing your psychic abilities and clairvoyance skills, to spirit guide communication, manifestation and tapping into your sixth sense, you'll have all you need to expand your consciousness, enhance your reality, and realise just what a gifted person you are.

You'll find many practical exercises throughout, because I know that real growth comes through action, so try your best to work your way through the book in order, implementing the suggestions as you go. This way you can fully benefit from each stage of a guided transformation.

There are many people out there who are passionate about helping us empaths to cope and survive. But I say to merely *'just get by'* isn't enough anymore. I want us to really live. I want us to *thrive*.

So brace yourself as I take you on a ride that could lead to extraordinary growth and a whole lot less overwhelm.

I can't wait for you to become the most powerful, happy and proud empath possible.

Let's get started..

PART I
UNDERSTANDING YOUR EMPATH GIFTS

PART I CHAPTER 1

WHAT IS AN EMPATH & ARE YOU ONE?

'*Empathy literally means to feel someone else's pain, to absorb and be greatly affected by their energy.*'

~Abdul Saad, Clinical Psychologist at Vital Mind

So you probably have a hunch that you're an empath, but what does it actually mean to be one? Is it just someone with a lot of empathy?

Not quite!

Being an empath means you have the gift to deeply feel and absorb the energies in your environment, sometimes even taking them on in physical form. This can lead to huge success and deep connection thanks to your ability to read and understand others in ways most never will, no speaking needed. Most people have some level of empathy, but the difference between having empathy and being an empath, is that you don't just empathise with people, you actually feel what they're feeling on a soul, and sometimes physical level.

Some other traits of an empath are:

- ✧ High sensitivity
- ✧ Being easily and heavily affected by energy
- ✧ The ability to feel the emotions of others in your own body
- ✧ Deepened intuition and a strong knowing of certain things, even without logical reasoning present
- ✧ The ability to easily make connections with animals as well as humans
- ✧ Feeling *'different'* from others or *'too sensitive'*
- ✧ Possessing a deep enjoyment of and even needing alone time
- ✧ Regularly attracting energy vampires or people in need of help

And more..

Do any or all of these traits resonate with you? If yes, you're very likely an Empath!

It's a gift that allows for deep connection and powerful intuitive guidance, but if the strong emotions that often come with it aren't harnessed, it can feel like more of a burden, as you probably know all too well.

This is because when empaths haven't learned coping mechanisms for harbouring the energy we absorb, or the deep emotion we feel, we can consistently live in a state of survival, stress and internal chaos *(we'll get to changing that real soon).*

A common misconception about empaths, and a common self perception of an empath in survival mode, is that empaths are weak, fragile people who crumble easily and can't handle life's pressures. But before we move forward I want this to be the first myth we bust.

I call this a myth because us empaths are actually pros at handling life's pressures *plus* the energies and emotions of others on a daily basis. Not only do we go through life seeing what others see, but we also often feel what others feel. And so yes, we might become overwhelmed and struggle when we haven't learned how to deal with those pressures, but we're certainly not weak - we're strong enough to bear the weight of the energy and emotions that we absorb *AND still carry our* own.

That makes us pretty strong *(and incredible),* if I do say so myself!

What else makes us empaths so special?

If you can't already tell, I'm pretty passionate about how amazing us empaths are. And that's not just because I am one, it's because I see the traits that we have, and I know that these traits can spread happiness, enable deep healing and have a hugely positive impact on those we share our gifts with. So aside from what we've already spoken about, what are these magical traits? If you're not yet aware of the magic you're holding as an empath, allow me to enlighten you!

~ **Healing Presence:** Us empaths are kind and caring by nature. Our high sensitivity makes us want to help others, and our genuine care can be felt by others as a healing and warm presence. This is a beautiful trait to have which can lead to effortless energy healing and providing great comfort to others, but it can also attract those who selfishly wish to overindulge in our goodness.

~ **Emotional Intelligence:** Us empaths are typically very emotionally aware and are also understanding of the actions and emotions of others, thanks to this trait. This can make us extremely thoughtful which again, is great! But our understanding nature can also cause some people to take advantage.

~ **Altruism:** Lots of us also have a strong desire to make a positive difference in the world and are highly optimistic. Our genuine care and concern for others can be felt by anyone we talk to and can sometimes attract nasties who want to piggyback off our energy for not-so-nice reasons.

~ **Highly Intuitive and Empathetic:** One of our biggest empath gifts is our intuition *(which we'll be exploring a lot more later)*. It allows us to understand other people without them needing to say much at all, which means we can connect with them on a much deeper level than most other people can. This can cause people to feel truly seen and understood, making them feel special and important in our presence. This, paired with our high levels of empathy, makes us pros at making people feel amazing about themselves. Of course this is a gift worth sharing, but it can also attract those in search of an ego boost at the expense of our own time and energy.

Although these traits won't be present in everyone, I have a hunch a lot will apply to you. *See, us empaths are pretty amazing!*

The Different Types of Empath

The purpose of this book isn't for you to strictly categorise yourself into a certain type of empath, but it could help to give you some confirmation and clarity to see which type you resonate with the most. As you read through the different types below, you might not feel you fit strictly into one of them, or you may feel you fit into a few. It doesn't really matter either way, but learning about the different types is a fun way to help you understand yourself a little more.

The 3 Main Types of Empath
(According to Dr Judy Orloff ~ Psychiatrist and famous Empath)

Physical ~ *A physical empath can actually feel the physical pains of others, for example if someone close to them has back pain they may feel it in their own body. This type of empath is also likely to receive messages from the other side via physical sensations. So if you've ever had a randomly warm body part, a tingling sensation on your skin, or a sudden ache or pain, your psychic gifts could be at play (we'll explore these later, and they're not as scary as they sound, promise!)*

Emotional ~ *An emotional empath absorbs the emotions of those around them. They can easily and unintentionally pick up on another person's energy and often holds it in their own body for some time. Emotional empaths often really struggle in big crowds, especially if there's tension in the air or anything negative happening. It can become incredibly overwhelming and draining.*

Intuitive ~ *Heightened intuition, psychic abilities and receiving messages in dreams are all common traits of an intuitive empath. This type has many categories from precognitive empaths, who have premonitions about the future, to animal* *empaths who can communicate with and feel the emotions of animals, and lots of variations in between.*

Some of the best artists, coaches, writers, dancers and of course healers who have walked this earth are empaths. Regardless of what type you resonate with the most, your ability to truly feel the energy of others and to instinctively know what they need, is a gift that seems like magic, but it's very much real, and it's probably the most common trait of any type of empath.

Take a moment now to think about what empath type(/s) you are. Are you all of them? Or very clearly just one? Maybe this self reflection will give you some *'ah-hah'* moments!

Empath vs a Highly Sensitive Person

High sensitivity is an innate trait of any empath. It's really more than a trait, it's a subtle superpower. The ability to truly allow yourself to feel is something that many people will never unlock. And if you can feel the full extent of sadness thanks to your sensitivity, you can also experience the bliss of true joy, excitement, happiness and passion. The ability to feel the highs and lows so vividly contributes to the rollercoaster ride that is an empath's journey. We'll get into how to feel more of the benefits and less of the painful side of your sensitivity later in this book, but for now let's address a question that might be on your mind; If us empaths are highly sensitive, doesn't that just make us a Highly Sensitive Person (HSP), not an empath?

Actually no, there's a difference between the two.

While HSPs and empaths share many traits, like becoming easily overstimulated, needing alone time, sensitivity to noise, lights, crowds etc, the key difference is that HSPs don't absorb energy like us empaths do.

They also often don't sense subtle energy shifts or pick up on non-verbal signs the way an empath does. Because of an empath's deep intuition, we're also more likely to have psychic experiences and deep intuitive powers *(all exciting stuff we'll get into later)*. HSPs don't tend to experience this so much, but many HSPs are in fact empaths *(we'll call those the lucky ones)*.

Though knowing the difference between HSPs and an empath isn't life changing, I hope it provides another little piece of clarity on your journey. Now let's take it a step further.. You might want to grab a strong coffee for the next chapter as I'm about to get all science-y on you.

PART I CHAPTER 2

THE SCIENCE BEHIND BEING AN EMPATH

Most of you reading this already know that being an empath is real, because you feel it deeply. But as with anything in life, there's plenty of sceptics out there who might dismiss the whole concept as *'woo-woo'*. Maybe even you reading this right now might not yet be fully convinced. *So what about the real science behind it?*

Though the research behind our empath powers is still limited, there's some great evidence to back up what we experience on a daily basis.

Let's get into it..

The Mirror Neuron System

The Mirror Neuron System is an exciting discovery that will have any empath-sceptic taking back their doubts. It's a mirror-like system that allows us to feel the emotions and mirror the behaviour and actions of others.

Researchers have found that we all have brain cells that are responsible for emotions like compassion, and these cells are likely hyper-responsive in empaths. This could be one of the reasons that we deeply resonate with the feelings of other people more than those who may have less responsive mirror neurons. Triggered by external events, these cells actually mirror the emotions of others, helping us to share another person's happiness, fear, pain or other emotion.

So an empath's common feeling of hurting when their friend hurts, feeling down when someone else in the room feels down, or feeling on top of the world when someone near them has highly positive energy, can actually be scientifically backed up to be real, thanks to the mirror neuron system *(phew, we weren't imagining it this whole time!).*

Electromagnetic Fields

Another very real and for empaths, palpable force, is electromagnetic fields.

Electromagnetic fields are one of the forces that can remind us of the vast power of the unseen. They're a concoction of electric and magnetic energy and are caused by natural phenomena as well as sometimes being man made. This force exists in the earth's magnetic field but also in phones, TVs and in every one of us, at a cellular level.

Empaths are typically more susceptible to changes in electromagnetic fields which is another reason why we can often feel overwhelmed due to sudden energy shifts. For example, some empaths fall into the *'Earth Empath'* category, which means they're deeply affected by changes in nature. If it's raining, they tend to naturally feel very low, if it's sunny, they automatically feel great. Or the elements could have a different, but still highly emotional and energetic effect. This is a prime example of being sensitive to the changes in electromagnetic fields.

This sensitivity to electromagnetic fields could also be a reason that many empaths prefer spending time alone and in nature, away from the buzzing, chaotic energies of the world. We'll get into how to protect yourself from this phenomenon later on, but learning that it's a potential, logical component of your preference to be in nature or in your own space, hopefully helps you to embrace that preference, rather than feeling weird or crazy for having it.

Synesthesia

Another interesting research theory is *'Synesthesia'*. This is a neurological condition that's caused by two senses being paired in the brain. It's also known as *'mirror-touch synesthesia'*, and it's what helps us to create multiple sense, rich experiences, like seeing a white light when we listen to classical music, or tasting a certain flavour in our mouth when we look at a certain food. Billy Joel and Isaac Newton are some known famous synesthetes, maybe you could be the next one!

This neurological phenomena is what could help us empaths to have deep emotional experiences like being deeply moved by a film, because not only do we physically see what's happening in the movie, but we might even feel what the characters are portraying to be feeling in our own bodies, or could even taste what they're tasting.

Think of yawning, it's contagious amongst most people. Empaths are just more susceptible to experiencing the same contagion from other stimuli. So instead of picking up a yawn, we could pick up a feeling, an emotion, a visualisation of a colour, a smell, or something else. This ability is just one of the empath gifts that adds more colour and depth to our senses, and allows us to experience life that bit more vividly.

PART I SUMMARY

So there you have it..

Us empaths aren't crazy woo-woo'ers, who have been just imagining what we feel. We're scientifically backed beings!

Though we know on a personal level that we absorb energy, feel others' emotions, and are impacted deeply by energy, it's nice to know that on a neurological level, these things are all backed up. And although we're mostly loving, caring people, I for one am not above wanting to prove the sceptics wrong, and you can do that now too, armed with this new information.

It's one thing to know that what you feel is real, but I'm sure you didn't pick this book up just for that confirmation. You want real solutions on how to deal with what you feel, and in the next chapter you're going to be given the tools to do just that. Start saying goodbye to your dear old friend Mr Overwhelm, and get ready to step into the world of peace and power *(it's much nicer here)*.

PART II
PROTECTING YOUR PRECIOUS ENERGY

PART II CHAPTER 1

ENERGY VAMPIRES, NEGATIVE NANCIES AND OTHER NASTIES (AND HOW TO PROTECT YOURSELF FROM THEM)

As the beacons of warm light that us empaths are, we often attract the shady characters. From energy vampires and narcissists to attention seekers and offloaders, it can sometimes feel like we have a *'welcome in if you'll drain me'* sign stuck to our t-shirts. And energy vampires are *(most often)* not dressed in cloaks with scary fangs, they're much harder to recognise. They actually come in the form of our friends, parents, colleagues or strangers, who love to sneak in and steal our precious energy. And the break-ins occur regularly.

In this book we won't dive deep into each type of energy thief individually because they could all fill up a whole book on their own. But the general common traits of all of them are that they drain you, steal your attention and probably take advantage of your healing energy *(they may not all realise that they're doing this, but some will be fully aware)*.

Cue unwelcome heavy negative energy and a lingering sense of overwhelm.

These energy leeches and negative nancies are everywhere and before we know it, our vibration has been lowered by absorbing the bad energy from the *(often well meaning)* nasties around us. Yuck.

So how do we protect ourselves and our energy from those who don't need or deserve it? By setting boundaries, *strong ones.*

Boundaries are one of the biggest struggles for an empath to build and stick to. At least this has been the case for me. But they're the only way to ease the overwhelm and regain inner peace.

When we think of boundaries we often think of physical boundaries; a *'do not disturb'* sign on our bedroom door, or an *'out of office'* on our emails - both of which are totally valid. But energetic boundaries are just as, if not even more important.

Really, we're all just buzzing balls of energy, and I like to think of the outer layer of our energy balls as our boundary line - the layer of protection at which we must investigate and allow or decline any one or thing trying to enter. Using this imagery alone can help you to detach from the chaotic energies around you. Picture a white bubble surrounding you that protects you from the unseen and unwanted. Only you can decide what bursts that bubble and interferes with your energy. People may try to pop it, it might be pushed and stretched, but it will only burst if you let it. You hold the control - remembering this is key.

So how can you become aware of who and what is trying to break in and steal your precious energy?

The first step is to become conscious.

It's very easy for us empaths to let energy leeches attach themselves to us without us even noticing. Like that one neighbour who takes up an hour each day confiding in us about her never ending tragic love life. Or that friend who always shows up unannounced because they need our calming energy to soothe them but doesn't consider that we need time to recharge and relax too. This is why it's important to take note of how we feel when we're talking to, around or even after being with, certain people. This is the first step in protecting your energy, because unless you become conscious about how your energy is affected by everyone in your life, you can't make the necessary changes.

So ask yourself, do you feel drained and irritable after hanging out with a certain friend or family member? Do you have to psych yourself up to spend a few hours with a certain colleague? Is there someone coming to mind that you just dread spending time with because you always feel heavy afterwards?

It's on you to set some boundaries to protect your energy so that it's not being wasted on people who don't make you feel good. Cutting out everyone in your life doesn't need to be the answer, but at least taking note of how you feel around certain people, and putting measures in place so that they're not draining you, is vital to your happiness. A good solution for this is *'time blocking'*: only allocating a set amount of time to hanging out with certain people. We'll cover this more soon, but remember that with any measures you put in place, you're not being a horrible person by doing so to protect your energy. If you're an innate people pleaser like me, it can feel uncomfortable to be stricter with your boundaries, but you can still be your lovely, loving, caring self, AND take care of your own energy. It doesn't need to be one or the other.

Another solution that's accessible to us all anywhere, anytime, is putting a practice in place to let go of any negative energy after you've been around people who don't make you feel great.

Here are some effective practises to try:

(You can use a combination or just one)

Exercise 1 - Releasing The Energy

This first exercise is a simple, effective practice for releasing the heavy energy you've absorbed from the negative people around you.

Start by taking in deep breaths, allowing yourself to physically feel any energy or emotions you've picked up, then release those breaths as you imagine pushing those emotions away from you. Make sure you're breathing in through your nose (because this way you'll absorb more fresh oxygen), and take as many breaths as you need to for any emotions you're feeling to settle.

Then remind yourself (outloud if you need to), that 'carrying the emotions and energy of others will not lighten the load for them. It is fair and safe for me to release them'. This practice not only calms your nervous system through the deep breathing, but it also lets your subconscious mind know that it's safe (and not selfish!) to stop carrying the burden of other people's problems, or their effect on you. It can be done from anywhere really quickly, so no excuses!

Exercise 2 - Strengthening Your Energy Wall

Picture yourself with a shield around you - this could be the bubble that was mentioned earlier, or it could be a shield of white light, fire or stones, choose whatever feels the most protective for you. Then focus on the purpose of this shield, which is to protect you and keep you safe.

Take some deep breaths and with every exhale, picture your shield getting stronger and less permeable. This could mean you see the light getting brighter, the stones getting closer together, the bubble getting thicker, or whatever else makes you feel best protected.

It may seem silly or even pointless to do this, but remember that we're all energetic beings with energy fields, so strengthening yours isn't pretending, it's real *(and it works!)*

Exercise 3 - Lighten Things Up!

In *'Empowering your Energy Field'* with Randy Veitenheimer, he details the practice of 'Logrolls'. This is an exercise that he gives to some of his clients to help them improve their energy, and it could be great practice for any empath who's in need of a raised vibration and gaining back the energy that was drained throughout the day.

All you do to Logroll, is lie on the ground with your feet together and hands by your side, and roll as far as you can to one side, then back to the other side. Aim for 1 minute to start, then work your way up.

The circular rolling motion and self massaging caused through the floor contact has increased the energy of Randy's clients and it can improve yours too. This may seem super silly, but it's great if it does! Do you remember when you were a child rolling down hills? The thrill? The laughter? What better way to bring back that inner child and get rid of negative energy through a *'silly'* exercise. The sillier you feel whilst doing this the better, because that will lead to laughter, which will lead to energy healing and a raised vibration.

The second step to protect your energy is to become even more conscious..

Further than being conscious of the emotions and energy you're harbouring, is developing the ability to decipher if they've originated from within you, or whether they've been absorbed from those around you.

As neuroscientist and all round incredible human Dr Joe Dispenza says, emotion is just *'energy in motion'*, and as you know all too well, that moving energy loves to make its way from other people straight to you. So being mindful when you feel certain emotions and analysing why you're feeling that way can help you to determine if what you're feeling has come from you, or from an external place. Only when we determine this, can we choose to detach from unwarranted emotions that we've absorbed from others.

Let's say you're hanging out with your friend and you start to feel really low. Nothing that you've consciously thought about has happened to change your emotion, but you've got a heavy feeling in your stomach. Without conscious examination you could continue to go about your day after you've left your friend carrying this *'meh'* feeling. You could get home and think it's *'just one of those days'* and your productive plans go out the window as you snuggle up on the sofa with ice cream and a film in an attempt to shake the feeling.

Or, you could acknowledge what you're feeling, and ask yourself if there's been a trigger that's come from a thought from within you, or if you've actually picked up that emotion from your friend. If there's no internal trigger for the emotion, or no logical reasoning that can solve it, it's very likely that you've picked it up.

And if you don't stop to investigate, you're bound to continue to carry it.

A situation like this is a prime example of energy vampires at play. Often without meaning to, they'll take some of your precious positive energy, and provide you with the unwanted gift of unease or negativity. Being conscious of any shifts in how you're feeling is the key in not falling victim to the vampires and negative nancies. Because once you're able to detach from the feeling and realise that it wasn't yours to start with, you can kindly bid farewell to it and focus on keeping your own vibrations high. Mastering the art of detachment is how you'll become a pro at this.

Detachment

Detachment can save you an unimaginable amount of energy as you'll be able to see yourself as separate from anyone trying to affect you. It might take some practice, but every time you feel your energy at risk, stop to ask yourself *'is this emotion mine, or have I picked it up from somewhere or someone else?'*. If you can consciously evaluate who and what is trying to steal or change your energy, you get one step closer to being in complete control of it and become a powerful empath who can withstand the energy vampires, narcissists and any other creatures attempting to knock you off course.

Once you realise that an energy shift or emotion didn't start with you, it's time to change your environment and attitude towards it and move forward. To do this, try putting yourself in the kind of environment you know you can de-wind in, or that makes you relaxed or happy. Take some deep breaths and say in your head or out loud that the emotion is not yours and therefore should be detached from you.

Practise deep breathing until you visualise and feel the anxiety, stress or whatever undesirable emotion you're feeling leave your body. Some great mantras to say whilst doing this are:

> *I'm in full control of my emotions and it is safe and fair for me to let go of any negative feelings I've absorbed from others.*

> *I am a resilient and capable empath who can easily detach myself from the emotions and energy of others.*

> *I am deserving of a truly happy life, and I release any emotions that do not align with that.*

Detachment doesn't only need to come into play when it comes to other people, but even our own brain can be a pesky little energy vampire if we don't keep it in check. Our negative thoughts can run rampant if we let them, and it's easy to forget that our thoughts aren't us, they're actually just part of us, a part that we can detach from and control, with practice.

Think about it, do you ever find yourself lying in bed dwelling in negative thoughts, bringing yourself into a low vibrational energy? It's on you to turn that around and set some more boundaries with your own mind to protect your energy.

How?

You can do this by firstly becoming conscious of your thought patterns. Catch yourself when you're feeling a certain way and do a quick body scan to determine how you're feeling. Are you feeling anxiety in your stomach? Stress in your head? Release it with some deep breaths. Remember that the emotions you're feeling aren't you, they've just attached themselves to you temporarily. With each exhale, picture any negative thoughts of feelings you're having, leaving your energy bubble or shield and bouncing off it if they try to creep back in. This visualisation will help you to stay grounded in your power as you get into the habit of showing your emotions that they can't control you. This power will strengthen each time that you consciously detach from them.

A question that can work well when the worries in your brain try to take over, is *'can I solve this problem right now from where I am?'* Most often the answer is a big fat no. So tell yourself that it's safe to let it go now and that you can worry about the problem tomorrow when you're in the suitable environment *(at work, at the garage, at your childs' parent meeting etc..)*. This technique has helped me and tons of others that I've shared it with with sleeping issues, as it's often when we're in bed that we let our anxious minds wander. It's a sneaky little hack because we aren't trying to combat the worry *(which as analytical humans, is very hard to do)*, we're just tricking ourselves that we're *delaying* the worry. And when morning comes we usually forget about the issue anyway, or it at least feels a lot lighter and we're more energetically equipped to face it. This isn't about delaying responsibilities, but rather finding ways to calm your nervous system and bring peace to your life whilst still getting things done when you can and need to - and not spending the rest of your time being stressed about having to do those things, which, let's face it, is just a waste of your precious time and energy.

Try thinking of your thoughts, and even your body, as separate from your spirit or soul. If you're feeling triggered by something, try looking at yourself in third person and making observations like; *'Ok, that thought has annoyed *your name*, let's give her/him some *useful exercise* to make her/him feel better'.* Doing this regularly will help you to look at anything you're feeling more objectively, which means a more logical solution is likely to appear and you can use better judgement to find solutions, rather than acting on clouded and heightened emotions.

We're all in control of our own energy and sometimes we're our own saboteurs. So practise mastering the art of detachment and don't drop your boundaries when you're alone. Keep your analytical brain in check when it tries to lower your spirit and don't allow yourself to treat or talk to yourself in a way that you wouldn't accept from other people.

Your happiness all starts from you, and setting boundaries from the inside out will keep your energy high and your spirit strong. It will also show others in your life *(especially the energy vampires and narcissists)*, how much you value your energy and how you expect to be treated ~ leading by example is the clearest way to set these expectations.

We'll talk more about boundaries over the next few chapters, but first, let's look more at who we need to set those boundaries with.

PART II CHAPTER 2

PICKING THE RIGHT PEOPLE

"The quality of a person's life is most often a direct reflection of the expectations of their peer group."

~Tony Robbins

Most of us grow up unknowingly being fed messages about who we should be, what we should do, and how we should act. Throughout school and into our adult lives, we act on these expectations, which often results in trauma that we continue to carry with us until we face it during a self discovery or healing journey like the one you might be on right now. And for us empaths, these expectations can add a heavy weight, because it doesn't always take words for us to feel them, the energy alone says all we need to know.

But now that you're here, I'm happy to tell you that you *do* have a choice about whose energy and expectations you allow to affect you, and this is one of the most important choices you'll face.

Elaborating on Tony Robbins' quote, who we spend our time with will heavily affect our life. Not just in terms of our schedule, but also our energy, emotions and ways of being. If we're surrounded by people who don't understand our empathetic nature for example, we could end up spending years trying to suppress our sensitivity and other gifts, leading to long term emotional struggle and a dimming of our empath powers *(which is what many empaths do - due to our desire to please others!)*.

This is why it's super important that we're surrounded by people who understand and truly support us *(isn't life too short to be surrounded by anyone else anyway?)*

Of course we can't expect everyone in our lives to completely 'get' us or our empath ways, but if you've explained why you need certain things, and have tried to put boundaries in place to prioritise your sanity and happiness, and the person you've shared with doesn't make the effort to understand you - you'll need to do some re-evaluating.

As you read this, people are probably already popping into your head.. Ask yourself how they make you feel. What expectations do they place on you? Should you aim to spend less time with them?

Once you make the choice about who you really want to spend time with, you don't have to hide from the people you don't, and you don't have to tell them all to leave you alone horribly. You just have to be more particular about your time. Manage it like you manage your money - it's just another form of currency after all!

It all comes down to remembering that YOU hold the power to make every decision in your life. You're the CEO who decides on the staff you hire and keep and the schedule that's most beneficial for your business *(your life)*. For us caring souls it can be hard to put these boundaries in place because we feel like we're letting people down, but actually by limiting our time with people that drain us, we're able to give them more energy in the time that we do spend with them - it's a win-win.

How about people that you can't get away from?

I know right now some of you will be cursing me for making suggestions that you literally can't put in place. Maybe you live at home with your parents or with a partner who you can't cut out of your life because you love them deeply, but they still drain you at times.

The solution is using detachment like we just spoke about, but also communication *(scary, I know)*.

You can solve helplessness and frustration through providing an honest and open explanation of *why* you need your boundaries in place and how everyone involved will benefit. The *'why'* here is super important. Most of us dread honest communication because it leads to conflict, which every empath obviously hates because of the negative energy that comes with that. But that conflict is almost always due to miscommunication.

So rather than shutting down and sneaking off to spend time alone, which could lead to your friends/family/partner feeling rejected or unwanted, simply explain that you need some regular alone time to feel your best and recharge. Pick an example of something that the person you're talking to enjoys doing, like watching football, baking, or going to the gym. Explain how your regular time alone is your version of that, it's what you need to feel your best self, and to give that version of you to them. They'll benefit by getting the happiest, most well rested, energetic version of you who can pour into them with all of your gifts of empathy, kindness and healing, rather than getting the burned out, niggly version.

Anyone who truly loves you will want to see you at your best, and if it means them getting an hour less of you every now and then for you to recharge, they should happily accept that.

Also remember that you're your own person before being a partner, daughter, brother, sister or parent. Us empaths often forget *(or don't realise)*, that we deserve to have our own needs met - make meeting them a non-negotiable. Whether that means telling those you love that you need some alone time, or setting a regular slot to exercise or meditate to expend some of the energy you've picked up, as long as you communicate that you're doing it to help yourself, rather than because you don't want to spend that time with them, they should understand and support you. If they don't, they're not for you.

Set a Schedule

Your task in this chapter is to get a schedule in place. Plan out your days so that you're in control of how you spend your time and energy. It's on you to make sure you have some structure and balance in your days, so that you're not drained by the end of each one.

This exercise might seem totally unrelated to being an empath, but as you know, some common issues we face are feeling overwhelmed, drained and like we're not in control of our own time and energy. Setting a schedule is a practical and effective way to take back both of those things and start reclaiming control of your life - only once you've done that can your empath gifts truly flourish!

Creating Your Schedule

As promised, let's talk more about time blocking now that you're putting a schedule in place. Time blocking simply means allocating set amounts of time to specific activities. During that allocated time, your distractions really should be blocked off; no email pop ups, no quick texts, no task hopping, just full focus on ONE task at hand. Your *'task'* doesn't need to be work, it could be meditation, breathwork, tidying your space or whatever makes you feel good. But the key is to keep that time as solely dedicated to that one thing, so that you can be present and make the most of it. This will allow you to make the most of your precious energy and pour it into the task at hand, rather than spreading it too thin by trying to do everything at once. Small time blocks of just 15-20 minutes can help you to get most of your important tasks done quickly and effectively, leaving you time to share your energy with others.

If your schedule changes a lot and you can't think of how you can create your time blocks right now, just decide on one regular time that you'll set aside as *'you'* time instead. Time is a luxury that a lot of us don't have much of, but even finding a non-negotiable ten minutes a day to enjoy some peace by yourself, can help you to stay in touch with your wants and needs, and energetically reset. If you need to, tell your children, partner, parents or whoever else might intrude on this time how important it is to you and set a clear boundary that you HAVE to have this time. Picture this like an appointment that you wouldn't miss - a non-negotiable. Who knows.. it might inspire them to take some *'me-time'* too!

Write down when this time will be each day and make this a new habit starting... *now!* If you can schedule in your time after each interaction that typically drains you, even better! That way you can make the conscious effort to let go of any absorbed energy and emotions that you've picked up from the people around you, and let them go before the next part of your day.

WARNING: *Your time will be at risk of being stolen..*

If you haven't already noticed, your energy is precious and highly desired. It's one of the reasons you find people oversharing with you, why colleagues and friends like to take as much of your time as they can, and why even strangers are drawn to you. As an empath you have a naturally healing energy, which is a beautiful thing but as we've already spoken about, can attract energy thieves who want it all for themselves. So remember that *'no'* is a full sentence, and remain conscious of prioritising your own time and sticking to whatever type of schedule you create, because you deserve to enjoy your beautiful energy, too.

If you find yourself struggling to pencil in your *'de-wind'* time because of other people's demands, ask yourself *'Why should I always need to be on the go, with other people, doing tasks I'm not overly passionate about in order to be busy enough to feel it's acceptable to say no to plans?'* The answer is *'I shouldn't'.*

So from this moment on I challenge you to practise setting the necessary boundaries that allow you to simply do nothing, or anything you like, by yourself, as a fair and valid alternative to plans that drain you. You are important and deserve to have some time to connect with yourself, your needs and wants, and there's no way to do this unless you sit with your own thoughts and spend some time doing things you actually want to do.

Here are some mantras to repeat when you're struggling to put these boundaries in place:

⋄ *Spending time with myself is a valid and valuable way to spend my time*
⋄ *I can provide the best for those around me when I'm recharged*
⋄ *I am in charge of my time and I deserve to spend it how I want to*
⋄ *It is fair and acceptable to say 'no' to plans that don't align with my values and desires*
⋄ *I respect my own boundaries, and that inspires others to respect their own*
⋄ *I trust myself to prioritise my needs and energy so that I can best serve those I care about*
⋄ *I am an energy healer that must reserve my energy to help those who need it, not those who take advantage of my gifts*
⋄ *This is MY life and I deserve to spend my time how I want to spend it*
⋄ *My energy is precious and should only be spent on people and things that align with my higher Self*

These affirmations, when repeated, can sink into your subconscious and help you to genuinely believe that it's safe and fair to set boundaries. It might feel silly at first, but say them as much as you need to until you genuinely believe them, then let them work their magic.

PART II CHAPTER 3

CALL IN BACKUP!

If you're a sensitive, caring soul like a lot of us empaths are, you might find it tricky actually sticking to the boundaries that you put in place to protect your energy. Those who are used to your people pleasing or caring ways could accuse you of turning cold or not caring about them so much anymore once you start being stricter with your time and energy. Which is why you might wanna call in backup. And the best backup is your *'why'*.

There's a *'why'* behind everything we do. We eat because we're hungry *(or bored)*, we sleep because we're tired, we laugh because we're humoured, we take new actions because we want to move forward and have more of what we want in life, and so on. If you can get clear with yourself about *why* you're setting certain boundaries, you can back yourself up if/when other people question them. Being confident in your own reasons shows yourself that you have the power to live the life you want, you don't need approval from others because you know *why* you're doing what you're doing.

You don't even need to explain your *'why'* to others, but it should be strong in your own mind at least.

To help with figuring out your *why*, any time you have doubts when putting a boundary in place, ask yourself the following questions.

(Remember that a boundary could be with people, your time, your space, or something else)

- *Will I have more time?*
- *Will I have more energy?*
- *Will I feel healthier?*
- *Will I have more freedom?*
- *Will I feel more fulfilled?*
- *Will I feel happier?*
- *Will I be more at peace?*

If the answer to these questions, especially the last one, is *'yes'*, any actions you take can be fully justified because ultimately, you're acting to protect your precious energy which should always be a priority. And yes, that's *even* if your boundaries aren't beneficial or convenient for others.

If you still feel as though it's selfish to prioritise your energy for your own benefits, think about some of the benefits it'll have on others:

- *Though you may have less time with others, your energy will be even more radiant and healing when you do spend time with them.*
- *The time you spend recharging your energy could help you get into a flow state more often, which could lead to ideas that could*

impact those around you and those you don't yet know, in business or in their personal lives.

✧ *You'll inspire others. It's common for us to live our lives for other people, but by taking time for yourself, to be your best self, you'll inspire others to do the same. You can show that you can still be caring, kind and considerate, whilst prioritising your own needs. This lesson will be incredibly valuable to anyone observing.*

✧ *You'll strengthen your gifts. Although we haven't covered just how much potential you have yet, let's just say you have A LOT. If you're drained and your energy is low, it'll be much harder to harness your powers. Taking the time to heal and recharge your energy will give you the best chance of fully tuning into your gifts, from psychic abilities, deepened intuition, energy healing and a whole host of other things that could hugely benefit those around you. So if you're not recharging for yourself, recharge for those in need of help.*

If you still feel unease and anxiety when trying to put your foot down, think about this too: In the Gaia documentary, 'Inspirations', Dr Neha Sangwan speaks about the discomfort you feel in your body when you're faced with speaking your truth. She explains that when we feel that discomfort, we often numb it with a short term high, like distracting ourselves with nice food, social media or ignoring the issue another way. This helps to distract us and comfort us at the time, but the long term price? Prolonged discomfort.

Keep this in mind when debating putting an energy protection boundary in place. It might mean feeling the uncomfortability of speaking up to have some alone time now, but should make it easier next time you need to speak up, and even easier the time after that. Which, in the long term, means less anxiety and better communication, leading to more *'you'* time and more energy. Often just doing these *'little'* things that we don't feel comfortable doing, like speaking up for ourselves, can lead to serious benefits down the road.

The alternative? As Dr Sangwan suggests, the more we quiet our voice the more we grow to respect and value ourselves a little bit less. Thoughts like *'why didn't I have the courage to say that?'*, or *'why didn't I stand up for myself?'*, will be regularly in our minds, which could plant long term disappointment within ourselves. *Yikes.*

Can you think of any times you've felt that disappointed when you sacrificed your time or energy for someone else's? How did it make you feel?

My challenge to you is to face the short term uncomfortability of prioritising your energy rather than allowing others to steal it, so that you can benefit from the long term high of actually liking yourself and feeling strong in your energy. Seems like a no brainer, right?

If you've been struggling to stick to your boundaries, whether that's standing up to yourself or to others, keep this idea in mind every time you're faced with a new opportunity to do what you want and need to do, even if it's not the most beneficial option for others. This is a tough thing for us empaths to do as we can deeply feel the energy shifts of others who likely expected us to go along with whatever they wanted, but setting and sticking to your boundaries can truly change your life and make others actually respect you more. *Give it a try and feel your self love grow!*

Activity: Next time you find yourself in a situation where you're being questioned, outright or subtly, about your choices, push yourself to stand up for yourself and your needs.

This doesn't even need to be verbally (because, like me, you probably hate confrontation), but for example you could demonstrate taking your power back by sticking to the time you said you were going to leave a social event, which shows respect for yourself and your time. Or it could look like consciously stopping a draining negative conversation to show respect for your energy. All of these small decisions are actually energy protection techniques that help you to become more confident and self assured.

Put the uncomfortable work in of setting your boundaries now, and enjoy protected and enhanced energy later as a result.

PART II CHAPTER 4

FURRY FRIENDS AND THE CRAZY BIRD LADY

Don't worry, you haven't somehow nodded off and picked up a children's fiction book in your sleep. I just have a little *(real and relevant)* story for you.

I was on a wintery walk not too long ago and I came across two little birds on the ground. *'Hello'* I said to them without thinking. And in talking to the birds, which some may find odd, a decade old memory randomly came back to me.

It was a memory of *'The Crazy Bird Lady'.*

Where I used to live as a child there was an elderly lady who would step out of her house and very quickly become surrounded by birds. Though I'd grown up watching Snow White and loved the thought of animals surrounding me as I communicated with them, my friends didn't see this woman in a Snow White kinda way. They saw her as odd, and so she became locally known as *'The Crazy Bird Lady'.*

Fast forward to my wintery walk many years later, and for the first time it struck me that this lady wasn't crazy, at least not for being surrounded by birds. She was probably just more in tune with nature and the feelings of other sentient beings than most, and had an openness and therefore a form of non-vocal communication with those beings.

She was probably an empath.

Animals don't tell you something whilst omitting the total opposite energy. They're pure, honest and as they are. So it's easy to see why us empaths could feel in tune with and understanding of an animal's moods and needs, compared to trying to understand complicated humans.

Are you someone who's drawn to animals? Do you find yourself enjoying time with your pets or animals you see on walks more than some people? Maybe you're an animal empath!

For years I've joked about being a *'Crazy Cat Lady'*. But the epiphany I had on this wintery walk was that it's actually not crazy at all to be totally in awe of, and enjoy time with animals. I'm not a *'crazy'* cat lady, and the woman who instinctively drew birds towards her wasn't crazy for doing that either. Maybe she wasn't an empath, I don't know her well enough to say, but it was clear that just like me, she found peace being around animals, probably because they don't suck her energy away the way some humans can.

Our furry friends can bring us so much peace, not just because of their genuine energy, but also because of their reliance on us. Us empaths instinctively want to help and care for others, which can be hard when a lot of humans aren't ready to accept help. Animals, however, often do need help, and our desire to please can be fulfilled by giving them the care they need.

All this to say that it's not crazy to stay at home with your pets rather than saying *'yes'* to social plans you don't actually want to attend. Of course human social interaction is important, but we spend so much of our lives surrounded by chaotic energy, at work, at the shops, at parties and other events in our lives, that taking some time to de-wind alone or with our furry friends can actually have loads of benefits and should be encouraged.

So if, like me, you're an empath who feels at peace when in the company of animals, don't label yourself crazy like I have for many years. Accept that you possess a gift to feel such a strong connection to our furry *(or feathery or scaly)* friends. Don't neglect that gift due to a fear of seeming weird or because of a belief that you should want to be around people all the time.

Just enjoy the gift!

PART II CHAPTER 5

ENVIRONMENT

Your environment is an extension of your energy field, so we can't finish this part of the book without taking a closer look at it. It's where your energy can either be protected or totally disrupted. And it's not just the people in your space that can have this effect, but even the objects, sounds and amount of space. For example, being surrounded by mess and clutter is only going to lead to chaotic energy. We don't all have the luxury of having our own mansions with vast space to de-wind and feel at peace in, but one thing many of us crafty empaths are good at is creating our own little oasis, even if it's just a quiet corner amongst the chaos.

I've been unintentionally brilliant at this throughout my life. Though my childhood was full of love and fun, it was also stressful and chaotic, and I didn't have some fancy feng shui'd space to retreat to when I was feeling overstimulated. Instead I'd take myself off to any quiet corner I could find to regulate my emotions and release the energy I'd picked up *(without realising that this was what I was doing)*, even if this meant sneaking off to the bathroom without needing to go. I bet you've been known to do the same?

But further than finding a corner to escape and detach in, is taking control of your environment, as much as you can. Clutter naturally triggers stress as well as sometimes guilt, frustration and other yucky feelings. It might seem like an overly generic suggestion to *'clean your space to feel happier'*, but it's effective and actually vital for those of us who get easily overstimulated. Creating a sense of calm and clarity in your space, even if it's just in your bedroom, will mean you have a reliable, safe area in which you can bring your energy back to a positive baseline, no matter how crazy the outside world might be.

When sorting out your space, also consider the sounds you're letting in. Whether it's the undertone of sadness in the classical music playing in the coffee shop you're in, the chaotic conversations of people around you, or the sound of your friend chewing their food, your auditory environment can just as easily distract or frustrate you as anything in your physical field. I've discovered this first hand through the feeling like my head's going to explode with anger when people around me are eating loudly; not a normal logical reaction, but one I just can't seem to overcome as a highly sensitive empath.

You may not even realise why your mood has changed if you don't acknowledge this one of your senses, but as someone who can easily soak up the atmosphere, you're likely to be heavily emotionally impacted by noise just as much as you are by physical stimuli. So over the next week or so, become conscious of the sounds around you, asking yourself how they make your energy shift, and try out some different music or binaural beats and take note of how they make you feel, then change up your daily sounds accordingly. Though we all have different personalities, likes and dislikes, empaths and HSPs can commonly be soothed by calming music, especially in the alpha range of 8 to 13 Hz. Try out some different sounds and take note of how your energy shifts.

Make it your mission to create at least one environment, ideally in your home but it could be anywhere, that you can retreat to to help you feel at peace.

What about when you can't control your environment? When you can feel chaotic energies trying to trip you up and the overwhelm is building with no clear exit route in sight? *I've got you!*

Grounding

An effective technique for calming and centering your energy, no matter how chaotic your environment is, is grounding.

It's a technique that's become renowned for helping us over the years to stay balanced and detach from unwanted energy. This technique can be done in a variety of ways, but let's look at a popular and effective method:

Step 1) Close your eyes and take some deep breaths as you root your feet firmly on the ground *(you can be sitting or standing).* Feel your shoulders and the muscles in your face relaxing.

Step 2) From your feet, visualise roots growing into the ground, keeping you strong and stable. While doing this visualisation, it can be useful to hold your heart or stomach as you take your deep breaths, and become conscious of your physical body and energy, which is separate and shielded from everything around you.

Continue picturing yourself becoming grounded, stable, strong and safe in your shielded energy field.

Step 3) Once you can see the roots planted deeply in the ground, envisage the earths' protective and revitalising energy running up through them and into your body. Remind yourself that you're divinely protected and in charge of your energy and body, no matter what chaos surrounds you. Continue taking deep breaths until you feel the energy shift you're desiring.

Once you've finished this grounding visualisation, return to the shielding energy protection method, and visualise your shield forming around you, ready to guard you from any negativity or chaos that surrounds you.

This practice can be done from anywhere and I hope it helps you as much as it helps me.

PART II SUMMARY

I hope you're starting to feel better equipped to protect your precious energy and are excited to take some steps towards more 'me' time *(you deserve it!).*

Because of the magnetic person that you are, and the warming energy that you radiate, there will always be energy thieves and chaotic energy trying to shake you. But you're now equipped with some practices that can lower the risk of energetic break ins and keep you safe and strong. Remember, if you're grounded and confident in sticking to your boundaries, you'll stand strong and intimidate anyone who's hoping to lower or steal your energy. I trust and know that you can put in place whatever boundaries you need to, and you'll feel so refreshed and proud once you do.

On top of using the energy protection methods mentioned in this chapter, it's important to learn to really appreciate your empath gifts as just that, rather than burdens. Once you do this you'll feel a confidence shift and will feel much more empowered as an empath *(and human).*

So if you're not yet convinced that being an empath is a blessing, this next part of the book should do it.

Let's take a deeper look at your empath traits, and say bye-bye to every empath's arch nemesis: That pesky Mr Overwhelm.

PART III
EMBRACING YOUR EMPATH TRAITS AND OVERCOMING OVERWHELM

PART III CHAPTER 1

EMBRACING SENSITIVITY AND ALONE TIME

A lot of empaths have two prominent traits - high sensitivity and a deep enjoyment of spending time alone. And though these traits are actually great gifts, they can often be seen as negative.

Sensitivity is often mistaken for weakness, and being alone is often mistaken for being lonely - misconceptions that cause a lot of people to miss out on the joy of embracing their sensitive side, and become scared of spending time by themselves.

So how can you work *with* your gifts of sensitivity and enjoying alone time to increase your happiness?

Let's look at sensitivity first.

I say sensitivity is a gift, because although a sensitive person may be easily negatively triggered, they likely also feel the highs of life a whole lot more than most.

'Why are the little things called the little things? They're everything', is a quote that really struck a chord with me as an empath, because we can be deeply moved by things that most people may overlook, adding importance and colour to what some may see as *'normal'* moments.

Maybe it's being incredibly moved by small gestures from those around you. Maybe it's feeling deeply emotional looking at a sunset, becoming highly invested in a great film because you feel the emotions of the characters, or maybe other things trigger your sensitivity. Whatever it is, I say it adds magic to everyday life. It's one of your empath powers!

Unfortunately though we've been conditioned to hide our emotions, which means running from our sensitivity. But what good is life if it's just.. *grey?*

Feeling deeply is not a bad thing. And as someone who feels all the highs and lows, my challenge to you is to embrace both sides. Polarity is what makes life interesting, it shouldn't be ignored or ran from. Not only do the lows in life accentuate the highs, but they also make it easier for us to figure out what we truly want.

Us empaths can innately feel if something is wrong for us, which can save us a whole load of time, energy, money and other resources. This deepened intuitive sense is a part of our sensitivity that allows us to not waste time on things, people and places that don't make us feel good *(if we can harness it that is, more on this later!)*

So embrace your sensitivity by tuning in to it rather than running. Really allow yourself to feel the emotions passing through you when you're affected by something before you let them go. Use those emotions to learn about yourself. *How do you automatically react to different stimuli? Could you work on how you react or should you make an effort to avoid certain situations and set boundaries like we just spoke about?*

Using your heightened emotions to learn about yourself can help you to figure out your triggers, reactions, and your likes and dislikes. If you're not convinced that your high sensitivity is a positive trait, then working with it, rather than running from it, is still the answer. The more you acknowledge and embrace it, the more you will come to see it as a valuable part of you, but not the whole you. It doesn't define you and when you detach from it by seeing it as a trait, not a defining characteristic, you'll be more able to not let it take charge of your life. The key, as with everything, is remembering that you hold all the power. If you're highly sensitive it's because you've developed that trait and it's become part of your identity, and you can recreate that self identity any time you like, simply by deciding you want to do so.

So rather than seeing yourself as someone who *suffers* with sensitivity, how about seeing yourself as someone who uses it to be in tune with yourself and better serve others? Who is gifted with this trait, rather than hindered or even cursed with it.

To become someone who benefits from and is embracing of their sensitivity, you've just got to learn your triggers and reactions, and analyse if they're serving you in the best way, making the necessary changes if they're not.

Use the following page to brainstorm about some of the ways your sensitivity causes you to automatically react to certain things. Then write whether those things are triggers that you could make an effort to avoid, or whether they're unavoidable *(in which case, perhaps it's time for you to work on your reactions)*.

Check out the example to help you with this.

Trigger	Can I avoid this?	Solution
I'm at a concert with a friend and the loud music and crowd is highly over-stimulating. My sensitivity is triggered and I feel irritable and frustrated.	No, because I love live music and I don't want to sacrifice this.	Firstly recognising the trigger and taking note of what senses are overwhelmed. Self regulating with some deep breaths and reminding myself that I'm safe and protected. Picture my energetic bubble around me, shielding me from the chaos all around me and giving me my private space to breathe. If I can't regulate properly, exit the crowd and enjoy the music from a calmer space where I'm not in the middle of the chaotic energy.

This exercise might seem overly simple, I know. But even a situation like this could cause a highly sensitive empath to spiral if they don't observe how they're feeling and self regulate. Maybe it's not lights and loud music that you're sensitive to, maybe it's people talking to you in a certain way, or something else. Have a think and do some brainstorming on the next page.

Your Turn!

Trigger	Can I avoid this?	Solution

This is an effective exercise because it puts you in control of your emotions rather than being a victim of your sensitive nature. There will always be external triggers and sometimes setting boundaries isn't enough, so preparing to handle situations with the techniques that help you the most, will mean you're not caught off guard and drained of your energy. Give this a go and make sure to implement what you've written in the *'solution'* boxes in your next overwhelming interactions. When you feel yourself being triggered, refer back to this exercise and see if you can react differently than you usually would. The more you do this, the more you'll realise your power and the control you have over your own emotions and sensitivity.

So what about spending time alone?

'Awwwww' my mum will often say when I tell her I've just been to a cafe or dinner by myself. She naturally feels sorry for me for doing an activity alone. But the truth is, alone time is absolute bliss to me, and I know most empaths feel the same.

This enjoyment of alone time doesn't mean we're miserable creatures who hate people *(well, maybe some of us are, but that's another issue for another book)*.. It just means we like our peace! And we often need to be alone to let go of the energies we've picked up throughout the day.

The good news is that there's a lot of benefits to loving alone time.

The first being that it's a chance to really connect with our inner being, with what we truly want, like and dislike. *You* are who you spend the most of your time with, so it's important to actually get to know yourself, to reflect on what you like and on how you want your life to look. Does comfort make you happiest? Or excitement and thrills? *Seek more of whatever comes to mind.*

To actually feel comfort in your alone-ness is also something that most people will struggle to ever feel, hence the many marriages that happen for the sake of company rather than love, or the many 'friendships' that are dragged out by people who don't have the same views or overly enjoy eachothers company anymore. Our enjoyment of riding solo is actually a great perk as we don't need superficial fillers in our life.

Many people go through life scared to hold this quiet space to talk to themselves in, and wait until they have a later life crisis to realise that they've been so busy living how they thought they should, that they don't actually really know who they are or what they want.

So embrace your gift of enjoying time alone by using it to look inwards; *no life crisis needed!*

A great way to look inwards is through journaling. *'UGH really? Another patronising person telling me to journal to solve all my problems',* is exactly what I thought when another author recommended I journal, so no hard feelings if you just thought the same. But that was before I actually learned how to do it effectively.

If you use purposeful journaling prompts and spend even just 5-10 minutes a day writing to yourself in a non-judgemental way, it can truly be life changing. So although it seems like a generic suggestion, I urge you to at least give it a go.

Here are some prompts that have been specifically selected to help us empaths with everything from emotional overwhelm and negative energy absorption, to high sensitivity and more. They've been transformational for me and I hope they will be for you, too.

Try using at least one of these each day for the next 21 days and you could experience some life changing shifts. Thank me later!:

- What made me happy today? Could I do more of that thing regularly?
- What has triggered me recently? Why?
- Can I think of a place that would make me feel totally at peace? Can I bring aspects of that place into my current physical environment?
- Whose energy have I picked up on recently? *(You can let it go now)*.
- What emotions am I feeling right now? Where am I feeling them? Are they even mine, or have I absorbed them from someone else?
- What can I do right now to let go of any negative energy that I've picked up?
- What things in my life make my energy feel good? If nothing, what can I try that could bring me more happiness?
- What are 3 things I like about myself?
- What are 5 things I'm grateful for?
- What emotions am I trying to avoid right now? What's the worst thing that will happen if I just face them, then release them?
- Have I spoken to myself like I would speak to a friend today?
- What relationships are serving me in a positive way right now?
- How have I given to other people today? Could I give more tomorrow whilst saving energy for myself?

By regularly checking in with yourself through journaling you'll be strengthening your relationship with your Self and will become more unshakable to the outside world. The more you continue this self-dialogue, the more you'll know, love and appreciate yourself, as you'll be making the effort to talk to yourself like you would someone you really care about.

There's a never ending list of things you could journal about, but the above prompts have been specifically selected to help with emotional and energetic overwhelm and to assist you in really getting to know yourself. Start and finish every journaling session with some deep breaths, allowing yourself to acknowledge any tension, anxiety or unfavourable energies you're carrying, and let them go on your exhales. Repeat your deep breaths until whatever feelings have clung onto you become less potent.

If you can harness enough self love and independence through getting to know yourself during your alone time, you won't need to rely on anyone else but yourself for your happiness. At that point the world is yours - you can do, go or be anything and external circumstances won't be able to persuade you otherwise. *That sounds like a pretty exciting place to be, right?*

"Empaths have often been labelled as 'overly sensitive' and told to 'get a thicker skin.' As children and adults, we are shamed for our sensitivities rather than supported. But at this point in my life, I wouldn't give up being an empath for anything. It lets me sense the secrets of the universe and know passion beyond my wildest dreams."

~ Judith Orloff

SPEAKING OF WILDEST DREAMS

One of mine has always been to write this book. To have it help other Empaths just like other resources have helped me. And you can help me with my mission.. If you're willing of course!

By leaving a review for this book on Amazon, you'll help other empaths on their journey to gain clarity and learn methods to help them embrace their gifts. You could also introduce them to TheMagicWithin community, where a whole world of support and friendship awaits.

We still have a whole lot to cover, so you can always update your review after you've left it if you read more that you'd like to tell others about.

Just go back to this book on Amazon to leave your rating/review.

Thank you in advance if you choose to do this, it means the whole world to me as an independent author trying to spread some of my magic.

(P.s, It's free to review and shouldn't take more than 60 seconds)

PART III CHAPTER 2

FINDING AN OUTLET FOR YOUR ROLLERCOASTER OF EMOTIONS

As an empath, the cycle of feeling and releasing emotions can be overwhelming and tiring, as you probably know all too well. Add in your regular side gig of getting drawn into helping others, and you're probably left feeling overworked and under-energised.

Of course feeling deeply and helping others aren't things that we should stop, they're part of our superpower! But we should make sure that we're able to do those things without losing sight of *us*. Of our own needs, passions and emotions. Maybe you've already forgotten what yours are, which is totally normal. *But it's time to get that spark back.*

So how can you channel your emotions and soaked up energy in ways that could awaken a passion within you or offer you relief? By being creative!

Before you slam this book shut because you didn't come here to be told you need to become an artist to solve all of your problems, hear me out please *(thank you)*.

Being creative isn't about becoming a popstar or expert portrait painter *(although both of those things are totally possible)*. It's simply *'the ability to create something new through the use of your imagination, mind, and experiences'*. It can be messy and raw, because it's about the process, not the outcome.

If you're someone who carries a lot of energy and emotions, getting creative could be a super effective way of transferring that weight onto something outside of you, making things lighter for you.

We've touched on the outlet of journaling and we'll touch on many more methods later, but this is an option that's definitely worth exploring, because it's known to help millions of people worldwide become happier. It might convince you to know that a lot of empaths tend to be successful artists, writers or other creatives, like the talented Joss Stone, who has been quoted saying, *"My mom used to call me her little empath. I just feel other people's love and other people's pain very, very easily."* And a great outlet for pain, and passion, is through art or other creative methods - especially for us introverted empaths who sometimes get tired of using our voice for expression.

Some empaths will find a great energetic release when painting their frustrations through deep colours in abstract art. Others will find it through dancing away their sadness to moving songs, allowing the tension to dissipate from their stomach through to the tips of their fingers and toes before they let it go. Others through singing love songs to expend the built up energy through their voice *(I've been known to use this method, which has undoubtedly been very painful for my neighbours).*

Maybe you don't enjoy any of these activities, but what I'm sure you will enjoy is offloading some of the weight you carry, in whatever way suits you best.

Some of the creative outlets you try will help you, others may be useless, that's ok. Only you can figure out what works for you. My only ask is that you try something, because it just might drastically improve your life as an empath

Activity:

Pick an old creative hobby or a new one, and explore it next time you feel yourself holding a lot of emotion or overthinking.

It may take some trial and error to find something that you truly enjoy, but any time spent on discovering new ways to make yourself happy is never time wasted.

If you're not sure where to start, try something active, like dancing, gardening or even just hiking! If you know you find some activities to be more of a chore or necessity, try something that you normally wouldn't allow yourself to spend time on as you don't see it as productive, like knitting, drawing or crafting.

During this process, remember that not everything you do has to be 'productive' in terms of working towards a goal. In fact, sometimes the most productive thing you can actually do is give yourself time to express or offload your emotions and cleanse your energy so that you can focus on everything else in your life with a clear mind.

Giving yourself time to explore and find new passions will also teach you that you deserve to have quality time. That you don't deserve to simply

live for everyone else and help them to achieve their happiness without discovering what adds to yours.

Your task before helping others is now to help yourself achieve more joy first. Remember that only when you're whole and happy can you help others in the most impactful way. So start serving yourself and experiment with some creative outlets until you find one that brings you some peace. Who knows, you could be the next big artist just sitting on your talents!

And if you're really struggling to find a creative outlet..

Start with walking!

Walking is a massively under prescribed drug for depression, anxiety and general sadness. It almost seems too simple to be effective. But as an empath, the joy that can be produced from being in nature, away from big crowds and lots of noise, is pure bliss.

Not only has vitamin D been scientifically proven to regulate our mood, but just being in fresh, open air with some sunlight on your face can massively lift the weight off an empath who feels crushed by daily lack of space.

Here's an effective walking visualisation for removing negative energy and overwhelm:

✧ Picture the breeze blowing off the previously absorbed energies until your spirit feels clean and light.
✧ Picture the air nourishing and cleansing you of the heavy emotions of others.

✧ *Allow it to reset you, leaving you to only carry your own thoughts and feelings.*
✧ *Take long, deep breaths as you calm your nervous system and allow it to return to a state of peace.*
✧ *Continue those breaths and allow any feelings of anxiety or tension to dissipate into the breeze.*
✧ *With each step you take, tell yourself that you're a step further away from chaos and any emotions that don't align with you.*
✧ *As you continue walking forward, tell yourself that you're travelling along the right path, leading you to comfort, emotions and energy that are aligned with your highest good.*
✧ *Keep walking for as long as you can, or need to, until you feel at ease.*

As an empath I often find it hard to think creatively in spaces where lots of people are present, and it's on long solo walks that my best ideas come to me. Maybe it will be the same for you.

Before you move on from this chapter, schedule in some time over the coming days to explore a creative outlet, or to simply go for a walk *(which could help you think of your chosen outlet)*. This simple commitment to a new habit could unlock a coping mechanism that could lead to huge positive shifts, or discovery of a hidden talent.

I'd say that makes it worth a try?

PART III CHAPTER 3

USE YOUR GIFTS TO HELP OTHERS

'*Generally Empaths have a mission in life to help alleviate suffering*'

~ Lee Harris, Gaia

No one likes to suffer, *obviously*. But for us empaths, watching another person in any type of pain can be more torturous than experiencing our own struggle. And unfortunately there's no shortage of pain and chaos these days.

With the increase in negativity comes the rise of people hardening, withdrawing and fighting. It seems like more people are turning towards anger and hate, rather than towards love. *And this is why YOU are needed now more than ever.*

Your empath superpower of being drawn to those who need help, as well as being a natural energy healer, can really change the world, one person at a time. If you're anything like me and a lot of us empaths, you're likely also an innate people pleaser, who gets real satisfaction from helping others. When this is a prominent trait of yours, it's important to remember to protect your own energy first, using boundaries and the other energy protection techniques that we've spoken about, before serving others.

Remember that your natural healing energy alone is a gift, and that many people will automatically feel more at peace in your presence without you even needing to take much action. You don't need to do extravagant gestures to make someone feel better, you just need to be you; open, a great listener, and ready to share *(but not fully expend)*, your calming and healing energy. With all of your goodness, you'll attract a lot of people to you as we've previously spoken about, so remember to be picky about who you allow to take up your energy.

But for those people who you do genuinely care for, and who deserve to bask in your light, let's look at some practical ways that you can really make a difference, and please yourself in the process.

Words Of Praise

Firstly, you can help heal those around you by simply pointing out their strengths and making them feel special. This might seem too simple to be effective, but so often in life the things we get wrong are highlighted over the good. Not always in a malicious way, but because of how much more noticeable a mistake is when you typically get things right. Colleagues, friends and family members are often too busy to notice the little things that others do well on a daily basis, so unless each person stops to praise themselves, it's very possible that they don't realise how great they're doing, or how important they are to those around them.

So that's where you come in.

As someone who likely gets energised from making others feel good, it's a win-win for you to give out some honest compliments to your co-workers, friends and family. There's nothing to lose and so much to gain from telling someone if they're doing something well, or even just that they generally make you happier. By simply bringing some positivity into a working environment for example, you could start a ripple effect that could change the whole company culture. Your words hold a lot of power, so start becoming conscious of how you're using them, and make it a mission to tell someone something nice about them every day. This will shift your own energy, as well as theirs.

Not only will speaking positively cause an energy shift on a local, instant level, but if people receive positive reinforcement, they're likely to feel more confident in themselves. And if they're feeling more confident in themselves they're likely to feel happier, and have less feelings of jealousy, resentment etc.. They're therefore more likely to compliment others, because they're less insecure and because they feel good and naturally want to spread that goodness, and so another person will reap the benefits of being complimented, having the same effects, and so on.. All this to say that your empath gifts of a caring nature and a desire to make others happy could start a chain reaction that starts with your close circle, and spreads to hundreds or thousands of people, so *never doubt your power!*

Activity

Grab a notebook and start writing down each time you compliment someone and their reaction. It could be telling your partner that you appreciate them, telling the shopkeeper that they have great energy, or something else. The more you keep a record of the positivity you're spreading, and the smiles and energy shifts you feel as a result, the more you'll realise your power, and hopefully use it to spread even more good.

Positive reinforcement from other people can also be really moving for an empath, and while you shouldn't rely on it for your happiness, having someone thank you for helping or making them happier can really boost your own happiness and energy too.

There's nothing to lose by spreading some of your positivity and magical energy, but there's a whole lot of happiness and warm fuzzy-ness to gain.

Money isn't the only way to help others

"No act of kindness, regardless of how small, is ever wasted"

~ Raymon Grace, E-motion

For years I was obsessed with making money. I thought that only once I had this certain amount I'd be able to help everyone I cared about, and at that point I could offload the emotional weight I was carrying due to feeling the struggles of others.

I'm sure you know all too well about the overwhelming urge to help other people when you can feel their sad or frustrated energy. Even more draining is the feeling that you don't have enough money or resources to help in the way you want to. It's a heavy weight to bear, especially if you're highly sensitive.

And there's no wonder that us empaths want to give so much to others, when the act of giving is actually scientifically proven to bring deep happiness. In one study of MRI scans of subject's who had donated to charities, scientists found the mesolimbic pathway stimulated once they'd made their donations. Sounds complicated, but this is just the *'reward centre'* in the brain that releases endorphins. This example shows the real positive impact that can come from serving others. Giving provides the *'helper's high'*, so as innate *'helpers',* giving is a huge contributor towards us empaths' happiness. So it makes sense that if like the younger me, you feel like you don't have enough to give, it can be seriously triggering.

The good news is that it doesn't need to be. Because what clicked for me, after years of worrying about how I could make a difference, was that I could help the people I care about more by just being my best self, and being around more. Of course money takes away a lot of stress, but so does company and feeling cared for, especially when you're being cared for by an empath. I've had many friends and even strangers tell me that they're drawn to me and feel like they could talk to me for hours. I'd say this is my empath power in play, and if you're an empath, you have this gift too.

We're beings of light and warmth and by just offering our company, we have the ability to naturally comfort others.

So when the urge to help, heal and give becomes overbearing if you're low on physical resources, give by just being you - the great natural healer that you are. The receivers will greatly appreciate and benefit from it. Allowing yourself to feel the positive vibrations that emit from people you've helped with your time and energy will also be one of the most rewarding experiences you can give yourself - it's a win-win.

So give, give, give to receive!

Energy Healing

As well as giving your time and kind words to help others, what else can you do to serve more and maximise your empath gifts? Energy healing!

Energy healing is a holistic practice that can have spiritual, physical and emotional benefits for the recipient. As an empath with naturally healing and caring energy, you're likely to make an amazing Energy Healer.

To perform this practice, the first key is to establish a deep connection with the recipient. So find a calming and quiet space, free from distractions, so that you can really connect.

Once you're both relaxed, move your hands over different parts of their body *(touching isn't needed)*, and intuitively decipher where healing is required. You'll likely hover over an area with your hands, and feel a sense of unease, or even physical sensations in your own body, when that area needs healing. When you find these spots, visualise warm, healing light and energy flowing from you, out of your hands, and into the person, focusing on the area that needs help the most.

Envisage the blocks or negative energy dissolving as you flush it through with healing, loving energy. Remain compassionate and caring as you continue providing your healing shifts, refreshing your recipient and easing them of any negative energy they're holding.

After you've intuitively found the areas in the body that need healing the most, ask if there's anywhere else that your recipient is feeling heavy, and repeat the same process on those areas too. Then ask them to take some long deep breaths before finishing, allowing the positivity and love and light that you've shared with them to flow through them.

If you're wanting to provide healing or comfort to someone, but you're not in the perfect environment, or you're not physically with them, try simply sending love and positive energy their way through intention. You can look at them or picture them in your mind's eye, and envisage a light moving from you, and showering over them, gifting them with positivity and warmth. Though this may seem like it couldn't have much benefit, quite the opposite is true! It's a form of the energy healing practice Rieki, and it's been successfully performed by healers for many years. Because we're all energy, having energy sent our way can cause a shift regardless of whether we're in close proximity to the healer. Try it out and spread your warmth to those who need and deserve it!

"Too often we underestimate the power of a touch, a smile, a kind word, a listening ear, an honest compliment, or the smallest act of caring, all of which have the potential to turn a life around."

~ Leo Buscaglia

PART III SUMMARY

I hope by now you're starting to see, even if just a little bit, that your empath traits are gifts and not curses. Your high sensitivity can bring colour to your life, and your need for alone time is a unique trait that when used productively, will build independent, self assured foundations.

Not only do you have the chance to experience life more vividly as an empath, but you can also add colour and positivity to the lives of others, through your naturally healing energy. By just giving your time and kind words to those around you, you have the power to change lives and start a ripple effect of love and light.

From a new empath's common starting point of being overwhelmed and unsure of their gifts, I hope you're starting to see that you're on a journey of fulfilling your vast inner power. You have magic inside of you just waiting to pour out, so start by using the energy protection techniques in chapter two to feel secure and energised, then use your gifts for good as taught in chapter three, to spread your magic to those around you.

Speaking of magic, we're about to dive head first into the mystic world beyond the physical. A world of psychic abilities, communication with the spirit realm, zombies, mummies and more.. *Ok I'm getting carried away.*

But seriously, as an empath you already have the key to abilities far beyond what you might've realised, from deepened intuition to spirit guide connection, clairvoyance and more. You're a powerful being with the potential to enter a whole new world with your mind and spirit, and in this next chapter I'm going to help you do just that.

So grab your wand and cloak, we're going on a mystical *(but very much real)* adventure..

PART IV
UNLOCKING YOUR SIXTH SENSE AND DISCOVERING YOUR PSYCHIC ABILITIES

PART IV CHAPTER 1

INTRODUCTION TO YOUR SIXTH SENSE AND PSYCHIC ABILITIES

Both of these terms will have many people whipping out their *'woo-woo'* detectors or running for the hills out of the fear of being possessed. But as you're here I'm guessing you're at least a little intrigued by the world beyond the *'logical'*.

The truth is, neither your sixth sense or physic abilities are woo-woo. They're both very real things that every human has the ability to connect to, especially us empaths. We'll get into both individually in this chapter, but for now I want to reassure you that by learning about these things the only risk you'll face is becoming more awakened and open to vast amounts of power that you can gain through tapping into them.

If after reading this chapter you decide that the ability to navigate through life with more clarity and guidance from both yourself, and the spirit world, isn't something you're interested in, you can continue at your current level of living with no harm caused.

So I'd say there's nothing to lose *(and a serious amount to gain)*, by at least exploring the other side. Let's get into it..

What Is Your Sixth Sense?

Your sixth sense is the most undermined but arguably most powerful sense of them all. Some call it intuition, others a *'knowing'*, but however we refer to it, we all have it, and us empaths are especially in tune with ours. This sense is what guides us from right to wrong when logic isn't involved. It can cause premonitions or psychic occurrences and when harnessed, it can guide us through life with more confidence and comfort.

Much earlier in this book we spoke about the science behind being an empath, and a lot of the research mentioned relates to our other senses: Hearing, touching, tasting, smelling and seeing. While we can all benefit from enhancing those, we become our most powerful and awakened Self when we can tap into this sixth sense.

The good news is that you're already pretty tuned into yours, even if you don't realise it yet.

To prove it, just think of a time when you made a decision that didn't make any logical sense but you just knew it was the right one. Or when you were drawn to or repelled from a person but you couldn't put your finger on why. Or when you just knew something was going to happen but you didn't know how or why. All of these examples were you using your sixth sense. Some may call it a gut feeling but it's actually deeper than that, it's a knowing coming from deep in our core. We often try to dismiss it with logic and reasoning, but it's always there, just trying to steer us in the right direction.

We're taught to quieten this gift, or worse, to dismiss it and replace it with logical reasoning. But it's there for a reason, and if you allow yourself to really listen to it, it'll put you in the right places and keep you away from the not so nice.

In this chapter we're going to look at how you can truly harness its power to receive strong guidance in all you do. But first, let's do some myth busting around psychic abilities, so that you can fully trust in, and feel safe using both gifts.

What Does It Mean To Be Psychic?

The spookiness associated with the term *'psychic'* has most people scared to even investigate past reading the word. But the good news is that being psychic isn't all about ghosts, possession and other nightmar-ish stuff that you see in the horror films.

The movie industry has a lot to answer for when it comes to promoting unrealistic and fear-inducing connotations of psychic abilities. They'd happily have you believe that to be psychic means being possessed, or regularly exorcising the possessed, rather than just being awakened, deeply intuitive and possessing the ability to receive guidance from the non-physical. This reality doesn't get bums on cinema seats.

As a result, the world has come to view these abilities as something to be feared rather than appreciated for the gifts that they are. In this chapter, the aim is to remove the hocus pocus that shrouds this topic and unveil it for what it really is; a gift that, if harnessed, can be used to deeply enhance your empath powers.

Psychic Or Medium? A Guide To Who's Who In The World Of 'Woo-Woo'

To understand what it means to be psychic, it's useful to learn the difference between a Psychic and a Medium.

Let's look at psychic first.

A broad definition of the term *'psychic'* refers to an individual who is able to tap into information or knowledge that would otherwise remain unknown as it's not physically visible to every person. In simple terms, a psychic is a spiritual guide with deepened intuition and likely someone who receives guidance from the other side.

The term psychic has its roots in the Greek language, and the word *'psychic'* is derived from the Greek word *'psyche'*, which broadly means the *'human mind, spirit or soul.'*

Using their abilities, psychics can communicate with the spiritual world. They do this in several ways:

- Through dreams
- Through visions (awake or asleep)
- By connecting with the Divine, the passed over, or their higher Self
- By deepening their strong intuition

A psychic's heightened awareness often allows them to see, feel or smell things that aren't apparent to others, but are crystal clear to them. *Sound familiar?*

Now let's look at them in comparison to mediums, as the two are often confused. While psychics can communicate with the spirit world just like mediums can, not all are mediums. Instead, psychics' communication is more along the lines of sensory prediction, intuitive feelings and thoughts and dreams, rather than having spirits talk directly through them.

So how about mediums? And no, we're not talking about the size of your Starbucks order *(who ever only orders a medium anyway?)*. Mediums sit on the fence with a foot on either side - often feared by the physical and in touch with the spiritual world; they're a vessel for the dead to communicate with the living.

All mediums also have psychic abilities, and their communication with the spiritual world is guided by sensory markers and direct contact with spirits. They communicate with the spirit world via thoughts, meditation, or by performing seances *(conversing)*. We'll get into how you can tap into this ability real soon.

Although many mediums will channel *(which involves having information passed through them from the other side)*, they will very rarely live up to Hollywood's creepy stereotype. When they're using their gifts you can expect to see them with their eyes closed, tuned in, and focussed on receiving their messages with good intentions, rather than eyes rolled back, bugs crawling out of their ears and a growling old latin curse being shouted at the observers. So if this chilling misperception of mediumship and channelling makes you too scared to explore your gifts, please know that this isn't an accurate representation of this practice, and we'll get into how you can explore this realm safely in just a few chapters.

So there you have it, mediums and psychics are similar but not quite the same, and neither are as spooky as you may have thought, right? Are you starting to wonder if you fall into either category? *(hint.. You're very likely already psychic, at the very least..)*

PART IV CHAPTER 2

DEEPENING YOUR PSYCHIC ABILITIES

Have you ever had the feeling you know what's about to happen right before it does? Maybe the phone rings, and you know who it is before you answer? Before you think *'well duh.. caller I.D'*, I'm talking about when you can't possibly know something, and somehow you just do.

I'm betting the answer is yes, because of the shifts in energy I know all of us empaths feel. While many people call this ability pure coincidence, I say it goes deeper than that. It's actually our sixth sense and in a lot of cases, our psychic abilities. All humans have both of these things, but very few actually tap into them. In the case of us empaths, this ability is more pronounced than in most people; we can much more easily see, feel, or just deeply *know* things that others are oblivious to.

Fine-tuning these senses takes practice, but as you're already a step ahead of most due to your deepened intuition and open energy, there's nothing to lose by exploring just how in tune you can get.

But first, what's the difference between intuition and psychic abilities?

Honestly, not much. Intuition is a knowing of something without needing logical proof or reasoning. Psychic ability is the same, but with a few extra side dishes, like telepathy, clairvoyance and other exciting gifts that we'll get into soon. Some would argue that intuition is just the *'realistic'* or less *'woo-woo'* version of psychic abilities, others believe they're the same thing. I'll leave it up to you to make your own judgments.

Regardless, how do you know you're using intuition or sixth sense, rather than just wishful thinking or imagination? *'Because intuition makes you feel uncomfortable, fantasy doesn't'*, as author Caroline Myss so perfectly explains. She elaborates that when it comes to intuition, you get this feeling that you can't ignore, it feels uncomfortable but it gives you a clear push in one direction as well as some extra strength once you act on it. *'If you've done something wrong', 'try to silence that voice.. It will not leave you alone.'* This challenge from Myss is a seriously effective way to show yourself that you do have this intuitive, psychic power.

Let's prove it now; Ask yourself, what do you really want to do in your life right now? If fear and judgement weren't factors? How do you really feel about a certain person? Or a certain situation? You know all of the answers, deep down. Your sixth sense is right there telling you, in your gut, in your stomach, in your heart. You've just got to listen to it. Ask yourself one of these questions and if the answer doesn't appear right away, it will continuously appear over the next few days, through signs or strong intuitive feelings. The more you do this exercise the more you'll realise that you have all the answers already within you, just waiting for you to observe them.

And with holding the answers, you're holding so much power. Tapping into and learning to trust your intuition is probably the best thing you do to positively impact your personal, family and professional life. It puts you in charge with confidence and a knowing that you can figure anything out with your own inner guidance. *Feeling excited about it yet?*

So how do you strengthen your intuition and psychic abilities?

⬥ *Be receptive to your gifts.*

Accept and be open to your intuitive abilities by telling the Divine or your higher Self that you're ready to embrace your gifts. Say it out loud and entertain the possibility that messages are just waiting to be revealed to you.

⬥ *Tune in to the energy of those around you.*

This is something you're already a pro at, but I challenge you to take it a step further. Observe those around you, like you usually do. But next time, focus on how their energy is making you feel. Can you sense their sadness? Or joy? Are you feeling any pain in your body that could be coming from them? Pick someone you know the first few times you do this, because the next step is to approach them and ask them how they're feeling, to see what information you intuitively picked up about them was correct. The best way to do this is to actually ask someone you know to be your test dummy, and sit with you in a peaceful room while you test your intuition. This way there's less energy interfering and clouding your reading, and you can also close your eyes to connect more deeply with your senses; not allowing physical body cues from your participant to give you hints.

✧ *Predict the future.*

Before visiting a new place, try and guess how it will look. Draw a picture or write down detailed descriptive notes and see how accurate you were when you arrive. This is a really fun way to strengthen your intuition muscles and start predicting the future with more clarity.

✧ *Engage in activities that enhance your senses*

There are tons of activities regularly used by the spiritual community that have been proven to enhance their gifts. Different practices work well for different people, so try out a range to see what works best for you. From working with divination tools like tarot, oracle cards or pendulums, to energy healing techniques like Reiki, and different types of yoga and meditation, there's something for everyone, and I have no doubt that at least one of these activities will help you to realise your powers and enhance your psychic abilities.

✧ *Stop belittling your senses.*

So often we brush off our intuition or sixth sense as *'just a weird feeling'*, and we let *'logic'* take over. But there's nothing weird about your sixth sense always being there, just waiting to safely guide you. Listen to it, and ponder on what it's trying to tell you. If you have a seemingly random thought, write it down and look out for any synchronicities. Or if a thought or feeling pops into your mind, sit with it and let your mind wonder. It's often when you allow this to happen that you'll have your biggest *'ah-hah'* moments; when the answers you need *(or didn't know you needed)*, come to you. Lean into the whispers of your sixth sense and let it talk out loud to you. The more you do this, the more guided and confident you'll feel. Don't belittle it by ignoring it, it's there for a reason!

Using these tips won't mean that you'll suddenly be the next Mystic Meg, but the more you flex your psychic muscles, the stronger they'll get and the more you'll start to trust your abilities.

Game Time!

Ok, you've done a lot of learning up until this point. To avoid you reaching for the duvet and heading to snoozeland, let's add some fun into the mix. Here are some entertaining but effective games to help with deepening your sixth sense and psychic abilities.

- ✧ **Psychic go-fish**

Much like the children's card game where you try to guess what cards your opponent has, this game is about guessing what's on the page.

Find a quiet space and take a seat. Take a few deep breaths as you concentrate on calming your mind and eliminating any intrusive thoughts. Then hold a magazine or book in your hands and choose a page without opening it.

Try to guess what picture or scene is on the page. For example, ask yourself whether it's a child or animal or if the scene contains birds or trees. Trust your intuition and then turn to the page you had in mind and see if you're correct. In the beginning, this can be a little hit and miss, but with time and practice, you will learn to trust your intuition and you'll be seriously surprised at just how many *'guesses'* you get right.

✧ Psychic mail-drop

This is also a fun and simple exercise that gets more satisfying the more in tune you become with your psychic abilities. Start by guessing how many pieces of mail there are in the mailbox each day *(you can do this with your email inbox if you don't have a physical mailbox)*. Then try to guess how many bills or letters you've received. The better you get at *'guessing'*, the more you can add to this exercise. For example, you could try to guess who sent the letter or the outstanding amount on a bill you received.

Both of these exercises may seem like you're randomly guessing the answer, but the more you do them the answer will become less a guess, and more a *knowing*. The key is to trust in your intuition and you'll do that by repeatedly using it. The more you practise using it in exercises like these ones, the easier it'll be to use it in more useful ones, like determining whether a new love interest is good for you, without having to date them for years. And no more unannounced visits from the Monster-in-Law because, boom, your psychic muscle told you she was heading your way, just in time for you to head out for the day!

✧ General Sixth Sense Strengthening

You can take it a step further by asking questions about the future, through exercises like the ones above, or through just finding a quiet space and practising asking yourself whatever you're seeking an answer for.

The key is to be patient enough to *really* listen to what your sixth sense is telling you. It's always speaking whether you acknowledge it or not. So tune in and let it be heard. Carry a small notepad with you to make note of any answers or signs that you come across throughout your day to compile proof of your psychic guidance. The more proof you have, the more confident you'll feel in your gifts and the more you'll trust that guidance is always available to you. You've just gotta ask for it.

PART IV CHAPTER 3

DEVELOPING YOUR EMPATH ABILITIES INTO MEDIUMSHIP

As you now know, a medium is someone who can communicate with the souls on the other side, *the 'other side'* being the spiritual, non-physical world. It's time to face the fact that as empaths, communicating with this world is not only a possibility, but also a reality that most of us already experience, but may choose to ignore because of fear.

Does mediumship scare you? That's ok, it scared me too! Mainly because I've grown up watching *'Most Haunted'* and thought that anything with the word *'psychic'* in it meant evil ghosts that you couldn't escape from and a life doomed by possession - who wouldn't be freaked out by that?! But I hope you're starting to see that that's not what communication with the other side really looks like, it's a lot lighter than that.

We've already looked into how we can start exploring our gifts of deepened intuition and use our sixth sense for guidance, but how about taking it a step further? How about exploring our potential to become a voice for those who have passed over? *Welcome to the world of mediumship.*

While being psychic involves receiving intuitive messages about the living, mediumship is a direct communication with the *(physically)* dead. And while you'll want to refer to the energy protection practices listed in a few chapters, this activity isn't as terrifying as you might think. In fact, it allows you to tap into a beautiful gift - one that you're very capable of harnessing.

As a highly intuitive being you might even already realise that there's life beyond the physical. Some of us might've come to this realisation when we saw dear old Uncle Martin who died ten years ago, sitting at the foot of our bed. Or more commonly, we get a subtle or strong sense (a *knowing*), that something or someone is trying to communicate with us. This is our sixth sense kicking in. And if you aren't in tune with this sense or haven't come to understand your psychic abilities yet, it can feel pretty overwhelming and spooky.

This feeling of unease, paired with the fear of becoming possessed, put me off exploring my gifts for many years. This is your sign to not waste yours.

The first step in developing your mediumship abilities is to let go of the fear that surrounds this concept. Look at this way; you already receive messages from the living through energy transfers that most people aren't susceptible to, spirit communication just takes it one step further. And as long as you're using your energy protection techniques and always communicating with love and good intentions, no harm should come to you - only enlightenment and guidance.

Tips To Develop Your Mediumship Abilities

1. Eliminate Fear

We've just briefly touched on this, but it's the biggest hindrance that stops people from exploring their gifts, so let's dig in a little deeper.

Consider that it's often the fear of the unknown that makes us fear in the first place - so by getting to know your gifts and sixth sense more, you have much less to fear as you can get to know and trust your senses.

Also remember that everything is energy, and anything unfavourable that you feel when communicating with the passed over, is just negative energy, it's not a scary monster under your bed! It doesn't exist in a physical form and just as with the energy of the living, you have control over whether it continues to affect your life. Use the energy protection techniques from chapter 7 and remind yourself that mediumship isn't quite what we see in the movies. Until you relax this fear, you'll struggle to open up for spiritual connection.

2. Allow space to receive

A common misconception about mediumship is that you need to draw the curtains, light a candle, and be in the perfect environment in a decades old armchair for dramatic effect, in order to be able to connect and receive messages. It's actually a lot less complicated than that. The key is actually to do whatever helps you to prevent your rational mind taking over the most. So for some, meditation will be the answer, for others, repetitive daily activities such as laundry, driving or exercising will be. These activities put our brains into a more receptive state, as we're not overthinking about the connection; we're open, but not obsessing and letting logic take over. This is the key to allowing us to have deeper insight or channelled thoughts. This effort to consciously communicate with the other side can be called a *'séance',* and you can do it alone, or with others.

Try it!

- ✧ Choose your repetitive activity or find a quiet space and get started.
- ✧ Consciously invite connection by asking Spirit to join you without expectation or pressure.
- ✧ Continue to do your activity, or remain in an open and peaceful state, allowing your brain to slow down and not obsess over waiting for your answers. When you're in the flow and relaxed is when you're most likely to receive your messages.

Don't be disappointed if it doesn't work the first time. Sometimes, it takes a few more tries to get this right. It's about making yourself available to receive while in a calm and relaxed state. It's also important to be clear about wanting to welcome in the guidance, and telling Spirit that you would like to receive, providing an opportunity for genuine spiritual connection.

Once you feel like you're getting some answers or information through, you can ask questions to the spirit you're connecting with. Anything from who you're talking to, to what they want to tell you, to what their view is on a certain situation of yours can be asked. Have respect for the spirit you're communicating with but don't hold back. The more you ask and listen, the more clarity you'll receive.

Remain patient when you're first exploring this gift and trust that if you send the invitation, Spirit will join you, and your medium experiences will begin!

3. Examine Patterns

A lot of spirit communication follows a pattern that's unique to each individual. A voice in your head, an energy shift felt in the room, or physical effects like suddenly being cold or hairs standing up on your arms, could all be signs of contact.

If each time your experience or symptom is the same, it can help you to differentiate between actual spirit communication and things you might just be imagining. So take note of every potential piece of communication, and see if any patterns form.

4. Decipher where the information is coming from

If you have seemingly random thoughts or ideas entering your mind, especially if you're in a relaxed or flow state, they're likely from Spirit. This could be anything from getting a hunch to check on your friend, to a business idea that you'd never considered. These seemingly random downloads are often spirits trying to guide us or tell us something.

If you're deep in thought about a related topic before having a big idea, that's much more likely your own mind at work. The more that you can decipher between the sources of your ideas, the more easily you'll be able to recognise when spirit communication is present. Remember to always thank Spirit for your downloads when they happen!

5. Use all six senses

Spirit communication can come in the form of a feeling, a temperature change or sensation, a smell, an image in your mind, an unusual or sudden feeling, or many other forms. By taking notice when something in your body feels different, you'll be able to more easily notice the signs.

When you feel a symptom, simply ask *'what are you trying to tell me?'*, and you'll very likely receive an answer shortly after, whether that be in the form of words, imagery, or another type of sign. Your sixth sense is often the first one to tell you you're being contacted, but make sure you're paying attention to your physical senses too, as those can often give you the confirmation you're seeking.

If you've been to a medium yourself, you'll know that they often report having a pain or sensation in a certain area of the body, or that they're feeling a certain emotion. This is a very common way that those in the spiritual world will communicate, by showing through the medium where their pain was before they passed, or by giving them feelings of joy or comfort to let their loved ones know that they're happy now. So now that you're acting as the medium, take note of any changes in your senses, as it could well be a spirit communicating with or through you.

Activity!

Practice is important when working to enhance your medium abilities. Although once your skills are developed, you can more easily receive messages from those in the spirit world who you don't personally know, it can be easier to start with someone you do. Use the below exercise to help get you started.

1. Sit in a quiet space.

Noise and distraction when you're new to mediumship can drown out the subtle messages sent by those in the spirit realm. So start by finding a peaceful space to relax in.

2. Close your eyes and calm your mind.

Let your sixth sense wander as you calm your mind and focus on breathing slowly in and out.

3. Picture the person you want to speak to.

See the person you're trying to communicate with in your mind's eye. Visualise how they looked, what they sounded like or if they had a distinctive laugh or smile. Really see them as you remember them - in colour and full of life. Ask them to communicate with you. You can ask out loud or through intentional thought if you prefer.

4. Start freewriting.

Use freewriting to write down whatever comes into your mind. Don't think about it, just write. Let any thoughts, feelings, words or emotions that filter through your mind out onto the paper. It may seem like gobbledygook at first, but eventually, you'll start to see clear messages.

If you're struggling to feel connected, thank the person you're trying to communicate with, and tell them you'll remain open to hearing from them as you go about the rest of your day. Then go and do a repetitive task just like I mentioned before, as this will keep your conscious/logical mind distracted. It could be when you step away from focusing on the communication that it comes through.

If you don't have anyone in particular who you wish to contact, you can still do this exercise to explore and deepen your mediumship powers. Instead of vividly thinking of someone you know, let your intuition wonder as it shows you different faces and gives you different signs. There's a wealth of spirits just waiting to make contact with you - how incredible a gift it is that you can grant their wish.

It can take time and a lot of practice to receive accurate messages from the other side, but the more you try and remain open, the more you'll receive. Start by looking for patterns and taking note of what you did when you felt the most connected, then repeat that until you're easily able to connect and communicate.

PART IV CHAPTER 4

CONNECTING WITH YOUR GUIDES

There are many types of guides in life; girl guides, self-help guides, tour guides, doggy guides and more. But the type we're about to talk about isn't quite as.. physical. In fact they're not in the physical realm at all; you can find them instead hanging out in the spirit world.

It's thought that we're all intrinsically connected to those who have passed over to the other side, and not in the sense that we're all doomed to be possessed by ghosts and ghouls, but rather that we're all guided by those on the other side, in the form of Spirit Guides. Think of them like our mentors, there to support, teach, and cheer us on from the spiritual sidelines as we journey through this physical life.

What are spirit guides, and what is their purpose?

Before you learn how to connect with your guides, it's important to understand what they are and their purpose in your life.

Spirit guides are beings or entities of energy; highly evolved with the ability to comfort and guide us along the correct path. They're not there to influence our decisions or choices but instead to provide the necessary information and support required to help us to make our own choices.

It's thought that our spirit guides are assigned to us before we're born and that they are responsible for helping us live a great life, attain a higher Self and make life's journey easier. If we listen to them, they can guide us back into alignment with love whenever we go astray.

While the spirits of deceased loved ones may also guide us, they shouldn't be confused with spirit guides. Your spirit guides are aware of your past and future and use this knowledge when guiding, comforting or informing you. They are, in effect, your *'all-seeing'* eye. They're friendly, helpful, and quite playful too!

If realising you're never truly alone leaves you feeling unsettled and just a little spooky-fied, that's perfectly understandable. But your spirit guides aren't peeping over your shoulder, trying to see what you're looking at on the internet or poking their noses into your jam-packed-with-secrets journal. Instead, they're waiting for you to call upon them for guidance whenever you need it, through meditation, dreams, or simply by asking for them to assist you.

So how can you connect with your guides?

The first step to connecting effectively with your spirit guides is letting go of your fear. Your guides are friendly and only want what's best for you. They're there to protect you, not harm you. Of course when opening yourself up to spirit guide communication you can open the door for some unfavourable energies to enter too, but as mentioned, in chapter 7 you'll be provided with all of the psychic and energy protection techniques you need to avoid any negative repercussions, so there's really no need to worry.

Connecting with your spirit guides also doesn't need to involve any intense rituals or voodoo magic. All you need to do to connect is be open, and ask for communication. This is best done in a quiet space in which you can calm your thoughts and really open up. A prayer-type invitation can then be done by simply asking your spirit guide/s to make contact with you. Once the invitation has been sent, it's time to wait and listen, trusting that your guide/s will contact you. This is the tricky part because most humans aren't typically good at believing in what we can't already see, so many of us become impatient and lose faith when waiting for our spiritual support. But this is why as an empath, you're already a step closer to your guides, because your senses will be much more open and susceptible to their messages, and you'll likely feel a comforting or just unusual energy before you even receive any guidance. The more you accept the messages that do come through, the more easily you'll receive them time and time again, and that ease will keep increasing with practice.

So how do your guides actually communicate with you?

- ⟡ Through giving you strong thoughts or an inner knowing - stronger than subtle intuition or mental insight.
- ⟡ Flashes of light when meditating, praying or deep in thought.
- ⟡ Angel numbers or seeing symbolic animals or signs.
- ⟡ If you're free drawing/writing after mediation, the spirit guide can work through your writing or drawing.

- They can also send messages in the same way they send them to mediums, with direct, clear dialogue or visual signs.

And more..

9 Steps To Connecting With Your Spirit Guides

1) Ask

Life can be hectic, and we tend to forget to ask for help in the chaos. So first, make a list of the things you need help with, and then after prayer or meditation, kindly ask your spirit guides to reveal solutions or to show you the right path.

Some examples of questions you might want to ask are:

- *Am I on the right path in my relationship/career/lifestyle etc..?*
- *What am I not aware of that I should be?*
- *What is hindering my growth?*
- *What can I do to move forward?*
- *How can I better serve those I care about?*
- *How can I improve my current situation?*

2) Listen

Meditation quiets the mind and allows you to really listen to and connect with the spirit guides' guidance or messages. Meditate for 10-20 minutes, simply focusing on your breathing and the sounds around you. Allow any messages to come in and stay open to these messages, even if they don't make sense at first. If you can't find the space or time to meditate, just stay open as much as possible to receive your answers. I often receive mine when I'm mid-conversation with someone, or when I'm in a shop or driving. Your guides won't deprive you of your guidance just because you're busy, but you do have to stay open to receiving.

3) Write/Speak

After asking for guidance, a great practice is to write with your spirit guides, allowing your pen to flow across the page without controlling your thoughts or editing. In time, ideas, thoughts and solutions will flow onto your page, some of which could be channelled from your guides.

Some people like to use their voice to allow the guidance to come through, and this could work for you too! Just start talking out loud, and allow whatever words are coming through to be spoken clearly. This will likely feel odd at first, but it might just be your way of letting your personalised messages come through.

4) Request a sign

Requesting a sign from your spirit guides to indicate you're on the right track is one of the easiest ways to get confirmation. For example, think of the first thing that comes to mind, a name or song, perhaps a colour or number sequence. Let whatever you think of become your sign. Next, ask the universe to show you this sign if you are on the right path.

I've personally used this technique with my friend before. I chose a red bell, she chose a red fox, and for consecutive days after we had picked these signs we both saw them repeatedly. Every time I saw my red bell or heard bells jingling I giggled and thanked my guides. If you don't seem to be receiving clear answers to your questions, add this sign element to them. For example, rather than asking *'Am I on the right path?'*, you could ask, *'Show me a red bell if I'm on the right path'*. Give this a try, and I think you'll be surprised at how clearly your guides are talking to you!

5) Wait for guidance

Pay attention to the guidance you seek; it can come in many forms. For example, you might hear a song that resonates on the radio or spot a poster with a message that feels like it's only for you. Often spirit guides use family members, friends and even strangers to pass on their messages, so really listen and look at the messages that are all around you. You could even see something a strange amount of times in a short period, which could definitely be a message from your guides to pursue *(or not pursue)*, something. Be patient and have faith; guidance can sometimes take longer than we would like!

This is why staying open is key, because if you're only open to receiving the answer in the ways and timeframe you'd expect, you could miss the real guidance hiding in plain sight.

6) Be thankful and show appreciation

Thank your guides with a prayer of gratitude each time you receive the guidance you requested. Being thankful shows your guides that they're welcome and appreciated. It makes sense to do this because no one, least of all our spiritual besties, enjoys being taken for granted. Gratitude is the cement of a strong spiritual relationship - make sure you're full of it!

7) Trust

This is probably the hardest one. But try your best to let go of control and allow the plan that your guides have for you to unfold. Their plans will always be what's best for you, even if you don't initially see it. When you surrender to their plans, you can be genuinely led to better life decisions, relationships, careers and even health. I can seriously vouch for this and have experienced numerous shifts in my life after asking my guides for help. Often the shifts were triggered by events that, at the time, I thought were negative, but once the dust had settled, I always reached a whole new level of happiness and fulfilment. Thank you, spirit besties!

Trusting that when *'bad'* things are happening, it's actually your guides rearranging things for the better, can be really hard in the moment. But if you can stay open to the possibility that you're always divinely protected and guided, you can navigate through life with more optimism and comfort. So try to trust in your spiritual protection and embrace any changes in your life, because they will always be happening for your highest good.

8) Believe in yourself

Remember that you hold the power in your life. You are the creator and centre, so trust in your psychic abilities and your openness to receive, and not only will you feel more self-secure, but you'll also be able to truly feel your guides' support. If you're totally new to this *'woo-woo'* stuff, I know it can feel silly, or even like you're pretending to believe in the unseen. But you can even start by just entertaining the fact that this could be real, and that you really are guided and protected. Give the spirit world a chance to prove it's there and you'll feel it. Trust that you're deserving of its guidance, because not only is it there, but it will endlessly support you when physical beings can't, and it will help you to help others, too.

9) Ground yourself after every spiritual experience..

Tuning into the spirit world can create an inner energy shift, leaving you feeling disconnected from the physical world. So it's important to ground yourself after connecting with your spirit guides. There are several ways to do this, but I've listed some of my favourite ways here:

✧ *Take a calming moment.*

Sit quietly and sip on a mug of organic green or camomile tea. Its cleansing and calming properties will help you re-centre. Take some deep breaths as you feel the physical warm water on your lips and in your mouth, reminding you of your physicality.

✧ *Connect with the earth.*

Take off your shoes and walk or stamp on the earth; feel the grass blades between your toes and the soil beneath your feet. Studies show that grounding can reduce inflammation, circulation and a whole load of other benefits, so there's nothing to lose! Connecting with the earth will also help you to feel settled in this physical realm.

✧ *Become one with nature.*

As well as connecting with the earth through grounding, connecting with nature as a whole is a great way to get grounded. Find a quiet place in nature and sit on a rock or the earth. Close your eyes and listen to the sounds as you absorb the tranquillity. Focus on feeling the air on your skin, hearing the birds or the wind, and bask in the physicality of mother nature.

You'll notice that these practices ask you to focus on physicality. This is because when you're connecting with the spiritual realm, it's easy to become disconnected from the 3D, or even disoriented. Although I want you guided and enlightened, I always want you to feel connected, sane and safe. So it's important to reconnect with the physical 3D reality after each spiritual experience so that you don't find yourself feeling too separate from everything and everyone around you.

As you might've heard before, *'we're spiritual beings having a human experience',* so although becoming spiritually enlightened can lead to huge benefits, it's important to not become too disillusioned from your human side. Embrace both by focusing on all of your senses regularly, so that you can become grounded and safe, as well as evolved and spiritually developed.

So there you have it! You have a whole host of spiritual besties and protectors just waiting to hold your hand through life. Pretty comforting, right? Using what you've just learned I hope you start connecting with your guides and other spirits real soon and start feeling the rewarding benefits.

My challenge to you before you move on, is to start your spirit guide communication right now! Use the tips above to get connected and let the guidance start.

Your guides and anyone else wanting to get in touch from the other side have been there for you all along. They'll be delighted that you're finally calling upon them, so let them support you and wait for magic to unfold in your life.

PART IV CHAPTER 5

CLAIRVOYANCE ABILITIES

By now I hope you're starting to really open up to the world beyond the physical, and I'm happy to tell you that there's even more to be explored!

What if you could gain information about objects, locations, people or events without physically being told about these things? Would it make you magic? Maybe, but it'd also make you clairvoyant.

The term *'clairvoyant'* is used to describe individuals with the ability to perceive information from a range of sources through ESP *(extrasensory perception - AKA your sixth sense)*. Clairvoyance means *'clear seeing'*. Basically, clairvoyants can *'see'* without actually using their standard sense of sight. They can receive their messages in several ways; via dreams, visions, daydreams and thoughts. It's a pretty handy party trick!

But from the time we go to school, we're taught that we only have five standard senses: taste, touch, sight, smell, and hearing. Our sixth sense *(or ESP)* is the one that isn't so widely spoken about, but alot of us know is there. It's our ESP, that kind of *knowing*, that helps us to predict that something's about to happen, or that someone has certain intentions with us, without being able to logically explain *how* we know. It's also strongly connected to our clairvoyance abilities.

This sense is still heavily debated in the scientific world, and any mention of ESP has most sciency-gurus on the defence. This is probably because of the age-old enemy we know so well; fear, coupled with a healthy dose of disbelief. Most people don't want to admit the possibility of something existing that they can't fully explain, it's just too scary for them.

But the disbelievers aside, this sense and other psychic abilities aren't totally disregarded among logical thinkers, with some scientists taking a deeper interest. Take the Institute of Noetic Sciences (IONS) for example, whose focus is investigating *'transcendent human experiences'*. They examine happenings in the realms of mystical, religious or other-worldly experiences including clairvoyance, all using scientific methods.

And perhaps more surprising than scientific interest, is the real life government's use of ESP and clairvoyance. Yep, that's right, even the world's top leaders have been known to use these skills as a form of military intelligence to spy on their opposition, in a practice called *'remote viewing'*. This technique was used as far back as the cold war by *'viewers'* or clairvoyants who used their abilities to spy on the enemy. These awakened people provided information about events, people, places or objects that they couldn't physically see. So, although psychic and clairvoyant abilities are often regarded as mystical woo-woo, there are actually people in positions of power who clearly see their value and potential.

And it goes deeper than the modern day governments and scientists. The term clairvoyance has actually been around for centuries and can be found hiding in most cultures. For example, religious Hindu texts speak about clairvoyance being a skill or *'siddhis'* attained with great personal discipline and mediation. Buddhism also says that clairvoyance is spiritual awakening *(prophecy)* and the elevation of human consciousness that can be achieved with meditation and breathing exercises.

All this to say that clairvoyance isn't just some made up theory used to spook, it's a well known skill that goes back centuries and can be used just as effectively today to gain deep insight and wisdom from those who are able to use it, and spoiler alert; you're very likely one of those people.

A lot of empaths already know they're clairvoyant because of the way they deeply and intuitively feel things and receive un-vocal messages. But others might not know just how easily they can tap into this gift. Well I'm here to tell you that if you're an empath, you're already a step closer to being clairvoyant *(in fact, you probably already are, and you just haven't realised it yet)*.

Check out some of the clairvoyant traits below and see how many already apply to you.

- ✧ Seeing flashes of light
- ✧ Excellent use of descriptive words and metaphors that seem to come from nowhere
- ✧ Vivid daydreaming and detailed dreams *(that sometimes show future predictions)*
- ✧ Seeing shadows or people in peripheral vision
- ✧ Can easily and realistically visualise the conversations of others

◆ Can sense if someone is lying to you or others
◆ Predicting or sensing that something will happen before it does *(precognition)*
◆ Being able to gain information from an object or sentient being by touching it *(psychometry)*
◆ Being able to see and accurately describe locations or situations in your mind that you can't physically see *(remote viewing)*
◆ Feeling overwhelmed when surrounded by a lot of people

Do any of these sound familiar? Maybe only some do, which would be because there are different pillars of clairvoyance, each of which can work separately or in conjunction with the other. You may have tapped into some and not others, so let's take a look at them all..

The Four-Clair Pillars of Clairvoyance

1. Clairaudient

A calm voice that can be heard in the mind. It provides short, concise messages to the listener.

2. Clairvoyance

Images or scenes appear that can be seen in the mind rather than physically.

3. Clairsentience

This is the most common Clair. The viewer will have intuitive feelings about events, places or people *(it's highly likely you've already tapped into this pillar).*

4. Claircognizance

Much like intuition, claircognizance provides the viewer with instant information they couldn't possibly have known without their sixth sense.

How To Develop Your Clairvoyant Abilities

By now I hope you're getting excited about clairvoyance and your headstart as an empath to tap into this skill. Though the media has depicted clairvoyants *(and any psychically gifted beings),* as the stereotypical creepy and easily possessed Mystic Megs of the world, hopefully by now you're seeing that these gifts are actually not creepy at all. They're a result of tuning into *ALL* of your senses and using your deeper intuition to gain more clarity and guidance in this chaotic reality. It's a skill just like using your other senses to become good at singing or maths. And I know which skill I'd rather master!

So how can you strengthen these skills and become a master clairvoyant?

The first step, just as with communicating with your guides, is to become open. You have to believe in the possibility that there is more than you can physically see, and that there are messages just waiting to reveal themselves to you. Then, when the messages come *(and they will)*, it's time to interpret them through your intuition.

Here are some tasks to help you do this:

Task 1: Clairvoyant Journalling

- **Step 1.** Get a journal or diary.
- **Step 2.** Find a quiet place to sit and declutter your mind with meditation or some deep breathing. Our busy lives can often be filled with internal and external *'noise'* that can drown out our clairvoyant abilities - try to detach from this when you can.
- **Step 3.** Offer up a prayer of invitation, showing a willingness and receptiveness to any clairvoyant messages that may be waiting for you.
- **Step 4.** Then make a note of any images or insights that filter into your mind. These could well be clairvoyant messages.

Taking note of the images you see will enhance your ability to recall them and allow you to reflect on them as you decipher their message. Pay attention to any repeated imagery as that will offer a sign in itself.

You can also use journaling to keep track of your *'hunches'*; if you think something is about to happen, or you have a certain feeling about something or someone, write it down, and come and check your notes after it does or doesn't happen. The more you can see your intuitive thoughts proved right, the more you'll trust your abilities. And the more you trust in the messages provided to you, the more guidance you're likely to receive.

Task 2: Use your body as a compass

Our body is always nudging us to listen to our intuition. Whether we get stomach ache before talking to a certain person, or suddenly feel heavy, or light, all of these symptoms can be messages just trying to get through.

So rather than dismissing them as *'niggles'*, intuitively ask what they're trying to tell you. They could be letting you know that someone is bad for you, or that someone is experiencing pain. Focus on the area with the symptom and ask *'what is this telling me?'*, you will be given the answer, even if it pops into your head hours after asking.

Try your best to not ignore these physical signs. Often in personal, especially romantic, relationships, our body can clearly show us that our soul is rejecting someone, or that they're bad for us. We might feel unexplainably closed off to them, not want to be open and intimate with them, feel anxiety or just generally unsettled around them, or something else. If you can't think of any logical reason that you're feeling *'off'* around someone, listen to these physical signs and if they were words being shouted at you loud and clear. These signs are an extension of your sixth sense kicking in, and the more you acknowledge and allow yourself to be guided by them, the faster you'll be able to separate yourself from people who aren't there for your highest good, and find the people who will truly benefit you.

Task 3: Practise getting to know people before you really know them

Another great exercise for strengthening your intuition and clairvoyance, is feeling out someone's energy before you know any facts about them/have spoken to them. This isn't about judging anyone harshly, but rather getting a feel for their energetic signature before you know their personality and history. You can do this when in a group of people, by choosing someone to observe *(without telling them or anyone else ofcourse)*, and using your intuition to learn about them.

The more you do this, the easier you'll be able to determine who is genuine and who is acting as their authentic Self. This is something you likely do already as an empath, but there's no harm in doing it consciously and often, to deepen your abilities.

You could also explore Psychometry, which is the practice of reading someone's energy by touching an object of theirs. Hold or touch the object and close your eyes as you allow impressions to flow in. Accept them without judgement and once you feel you've got a well-rounded impression, write it down and reflect back on your reading once you've gotten to know the person more.

Task 4: Strengthen your other senses

Another tip to help you deepen your clairvoyant abilities, is to tune into your other five senses more. By really focusing on what you hear, see, touch, taste and smell, you'll become more intune with yourself, and it's then much easier to tune into your sixth sense too.

Task 5: Open your chakra centres

We all have seven chakras, that when open and balanced, we can thrive as our best self and receive clairvoyant messages with ease. You can notice different chakras being blocked due to different symptoms, for example if you're struggling with your sexuality or struggling to tap into your sensual side, your sacral chakra could be blocked. Or if you're finding it hard to speak up and voice something that you're concerned about, your throat chakra could be blocked. There are different ways to unblock each chakra, and we won't cover them all in this book as they could fill up a whole book of their own. But meditation, affirmations, yoga and mudras are some good places to start. For the sake of you being able to research how to unblock each one, here are the different chakras:

- Muladhara Chakra – Root Chakra.
- Svadhishthana Chakra – Sacral Chakra.
- Manipura Chakra – Solar Plexus Chakra.
- Anahata Chakra – Heart Chakra.
- Vishuddha Chakra – Throat Chakra.
- Ajna Chakra – Third Eye Chakra.
- Sahastrara Chakra – Crown Chakra.

Once you're confident they're all unblocked, you're bound to feel your very best, and will find it much easier to receive clairvoyant messages via all of your senses.

Task 6: Receive guidance through meditation

Find a quiet space and sit or lie comfortably. Set a timer for 10-15 minutes or however long you can spare. Close your eyes if you can. Then, just as you would when journaling, say a prayer or invitation for your messages to come in.

Keep some long, deep breaths going as you allow your mind to wander in a relaxed state. If you can stay relaxed and not be distracted by the outside world, you could find yourself almost in a trance state - where clairvoyant messages, images and other signs can flow to you freely without resistance.

Allow your visualisations to take you from scene to scene in your mind's eye, where you can see different imagery, faces, or could even hear different sounds or smell different scents. If something makes you feel uneasy, continue your deep breaths and remind yourself that you're divinely protected at all times, and mentally move to the next image or sign. This meditative state can allow a wealth of messages to pour through. Try to let them continue flowing without question, judgement or analysis at this point.

Then, when your timer goes off, write down all you recall about your experience, and reflect on what guidance you received.

If there's no clear message, that's ok! Reflect on your notes later or after a few days, and your guidance may well become more clear and meaningful after time, or after you experience more synchronicities.

When you repeat this meditative practice, you could also see repeated imagery in your sessions, which can act as a clear sign and guidance in itself.

Over the coming weeks, try out some of these tasks and I have no doubt you'll surprise yourself with just how in tune you already are. Your gifts are just waiting to be explored, start the journey now and let the guidance from beyond the physical trickle in.

PART IV CHAPTER 6

THE POWER & PURPOSE OF DREAMS

Dreams, we all have them, but what actually are they? Is there a significance to their existence, or are they simply the body's way of entertaining itself while we rest? Oneirology *(the scientific study of dreams)* offers many theories, one being that dreaming allows the brain to review and integrate memories and emotions while we sleep, helping us to process events from throughout our day. Another theory is that dreams are the result of unresolved conflict or tension in our waking lives, which often leads to nightmares or night terrors.

The truth is, us humans are still trying to figure out their real purpose. But one thing's for sure, we all experience them. And according to scientists, most of us dream for around two hours a night, with each dream lasting just a few minutes. So those mortifying naked at-work experiences everyone has dreamed about are actually only a few minutes long, not the marathon extravaganzas they feel like when you wake up anxious that Suzy from accounts saw you hiding behind the paper copier totally *'au-natural'!*

For most people, dreams lose their power with the rising sun. After a quick *'that was weird'*, the dream is forgotten, and the normal day continues. For us empaths, not so much.

If a dream has been particularly negative, illuminating or exciting, it can really trigger our high sensitivity, leaving us struggling to shake off the feeling that it was *'just a dream'*.

Thanks to our emotional-sponge ways, we're often holding onto energies and emotions that we carry with us to the bedroom. And if we don't confront them, they stay lodged in our subconscious, ready to play out over and over again in our minds while we're sleeping. This is often the cause of the highly emotional dreams we experience.

My personal experience reflects this concept to a T. Since my childhood, I've experienced intense dreams, just like you probably have. When I was younger, I would have consistent night terrors, to the point that my mother took me to the doctors because she thought there must be something wrong with me, as I'd scream and kick in my sleep as if I was being physically attacked. Neither of us knew that I was an empath at the time, but even if we did, can you imagine trying to explain that to an actual medical doctor over ten years ago? As much as healthcare professionals are becoming more aware of us empaths, many would likely label me with some unfortunate mental health issue, or gift my mother with a Child Services visit.

As a result of no solution, the lingering chaotic energy that often surrounded me in the daytime would come alive at night when I was sleeping. And it was more than inconvenient, it was terrifying. On the flip side though, I'd also have incredibly lovely dreams. The type that were so bright and vivid I'd often write them down, planning in my innocence to make a film out of them *'when I was older'*.

Looking back, it all makes a lot more sense; I was constantly absorbing deep emotions that the little me didn't know how to process. When empaths do this *(no matter how old we are)*, it's sometimes hard to think logically about the emotion we're holding onto and then let it go. This was even more confusing for me as a child because I had no idea where the emotion had come from or why I was feeling it in the first place.

Adulthood has brought about the realisation that I'm an empath, and through understanding this, I've learned to protect my energy and detach myself from unwanted emotions and energies using the techniques previously spoken about in this book. I still have very vivid dreams, but nowhere near as intense or unbearable as when I was a child carrying around the burden of unresolved tension.

I blabber on about my experience, because I have a feeling you've perhaps experienced the same, or similar. *So have a think, what have your dream experiences been? Do you resonate with some of what you've just read?*

If yes, before you go to sleep next, make a conscious effort to detach from any energies you've picked up throughout your day, and try to consciously process anything you've faced that you don't want to dream about, like an argument or anything that's upset you. I find that journaling about these things helps to get them out of the mind and stuck on the paper. When closing your journal or folding over the paper you're writing on, visualise the issue leaving your energy field and being stuck in the paper until *(if ever)*, you're ready to face it again.

Here are some more tips to banish the nightmares:

✧ *Meditate Regularly*

Practising mindfulness helps us process absorbed emotions before going to sleep and can prevent nightmares. Meditate for 5-15 minutes each day *(or longer if you can!)*, and make the conscious effort to calm your nervous system with deep breathing and relaxation. Visualise physically throwing or gently removing the negative energy/feelings of others or events out of your space as part of your meditation practice so that you're carrying less negative energy with you to snoozeland.

✧ *Remain Hydrated*

In many practices and cultures, water represents emotions and is the element of the second or sacral chakra *(feelings or emotions)*. Due to its fluidity, it's symbolic of the flowing and changeable nature of our energy and emotions, and as it's so vital to us, it's important we have a good relationship with it. When you're dehydrated, your spiritual energy can suffer too, which can leave you struggling to process absorbed emotions. So when you're drinking fresh water, try using it as a visualisation opportunity, picturing heavy lingering energy washing away with every sip, as your energy and emotions become balanced.

As well as the spiritual effects, lack of water can of course have a negative physical impact too. Both times in my life when I've had the most horrendous night terrors whilst lucid dreaming *(which we'll cover soon!)*, I've been dehydrated, so I can vouch for the importance of good hydration to scare those dream monsters away!

❖ *Use protective crystals*

Crystals have become an often overlooked and even sometimes mocked addition to a wellness practice. But they've been used for centuries for their beneficial properties, and they could really benefit you, too.

So try placing one or a few protective crystals near your bed before you sleep and see what effects they have. Not only can they protect you against negative energies, but they can also help you to relax and receive emotional and physical benefits. Certain crystals have also been known to help reduce the frequency and freakiness of nightmares.

We'll cover crystals in a lot more detail soon, but here are some of the best for protection and peace:

1. Moonstone
2. Howlite
3. Rose Quartz
4. Danburite
5. Selenite

What are our dreams trying to tell us?

So we've covered the not-so-nice side of snooze land and how to make it less spooky, but what about the other side? The magical and informative? Author and Empath Alison Alverson suggests, *"Carl Jung saw dreams as the psyche's or soul's attempt to communicate important things to the individual"*. I like to think of dreams in the same way, as well as them being a portal for spirit communication. Many won't have the emotional depth or openness to truly feel the messages coming from their dreams, but we, as empaths, do, and this makes vivid dreams one of our empath gifts. It's also well known that our logical minds can hinder our sixth sense and psychic connection, so it makes sense that being in the relaxed dream state is the perfect environment for physic messages to come through.

Once we've mastered energy protection and emotional regulation, we should be able to enjoy the perks of our openness and connection to spirit in our sleep, leading to lots of benefits, from less nightmares to more guidance. The messages we receive in dreamland can help us to make decisions or serve as premonitions for events in our waking life. So how can we make the most of them and decipher the guidance being provided?

While it's physically impossible to write down your dreams as you dream them *(unless you're an AI robot reading this, which is a very real possibility)*, keeping a dream diary is a great way to reflect on the guidance that you get in your dreams. Whether the guidance is coming from your higher Self, your guides, or from others in the spirit world, it's important to note down every message you receive, because even if they're not clear at first, there could be important messages trying to come through.

In the first few minutes of waking up, quickly make note of any emotions you're feeling, or any images, messages or events you saw in your dreams. You might not see a clear message initially, which is why journaling can really help you to notice any themes or signs of communication.

Here are some prompts to help you decipher the messages in your dreams:

> ✧ Were there any prominent colours shown? If yes, search the 'colour theory' for that particular colour, there could be a strong meaning there.
> ✧ Were there any symbols shown? What are the connotations of these symbols?
> ✧ How did you generally feel in your dream? Were there feelings of jealousy? Resentment? Anger? Are these emotions that need to be addressed in your waking life?
> ✧ Who was present in your dream? What do those people, beings or animals represent? If it's not clear straight away and the person/people shown seem totally random, think about their characteristics, and how they made you feel. Did they make you feel loved? Inferior? Or something else? Are these things you're craving or need to work on? Were they confident or anxious? Is this reflective of yourself?
> ✧ What was the environment like in your dream? Does it symbolise needing to change your real environment?

When deciphered properly, dreams can provide a lot of useful guidance. So start with these prompts and some regular dream journaling, and I have no doubt that very soon you'll see the value of your time in dreamland.

Lucid Dreaming

We can't talk about our sixth sense and dreams without touching on the unique phenomenon that is lucid dreaming. Lucid dreaming is when you can tell that you're dreaming, while still asleep. It can happen voluntarily or involuntarily, and when mastered, it can allow you to control your dreams, pretty cool, *right?*

As an empath who's in tune with your senses, you can use lucid dreaming to have extremely vivid dreaming experiences that can have spiritual, mental and emotional benefits.

One example is in a survey of 301 lucid dreamers, 64% used their skills to overcome their regular nightmares, while others achieved problem solving, creative exploration or spiritual enlightenment.

These achievements can happen through facing the emotion-inducing stimuli in the dream, rather than running away from it by attempting to wake up. This can look like having a discussion with the triggering person who's in your nightmare, rather than letting them continue to upset you. It could look like facing the scary apparition and telling them they have no power over you anymore until they leave your dream. It could look like having an uncomfortable conversation with someone until a solution is found, rather than running away from it. Just like how facing and dealing with trauma in our waking lives can improve our waking *(and sleeping)* experience, learning to process our dreams *when we're in them,* can help to stop destructive cycles in our dreams and our reality.

You may well be all *'sixth sense'*-d out by now.. but dreaming, and especially lucid dreaming, is another effective way to deepen this sense and make the most of it. When you're having a lucid dreaming experience, really pay attention to *(and take note of when you wake up)*, the intuitive messages and feelings that come to you. The more you listen to them, the more they'll show up, and that right there, is you becoming more in tune with your gifts, which will have countless benefits.

How To Lucid Dream

Enough of the what and why, let's get into the *how*. Lucid dreaming occurs during the REM part of the sleep cycle, which happens around every 90 minutes when we sleep. So the first step to lucid dreaming is making sure you get enough sleep to actually have these cycles, and also having good sleep health through limiting alcohol use, screen time, being hydrated, and being generally healthy. Easier said than done, I know. But try to think of getting enough sleep as your first priority, even if it means missing an hour of another important task. All of your gifts *(and health)*, will be compromised if you're running on empty, and I know it's annoying to hear *(especially if you have children etc..)*, but it's super super important to sleep enough. Ok, lecture over.

Once you have a solid healthy sleeping foundation, you just need to set the intention of lucid dreaming, until it happens. This is called the mnemonic induction of lucid dreams (MILD), sounds unnecessarily fancy, but it's simple and very doable with practice.

As well as setting the intention to lucid dream, set an intention of what you want to achieve. Do you want to stop a recurring nightmare? Communicate more vividly with your spirit guides? Or talk to someone on the other side? Go into your sleep with purpose to maximise your experience. State out loud or in your mind what your intention is, and invite your higher Self, or your guides, to fulfil your wishes.

Remember to be patient with this process as you are with all of your gifts, as it can take a few tries to have a vivid lucid dreaming experience *(although sometimes, it will happen without any intention at all!)*

Summary

So you now have some tips and tricks to help you maximise your gifts not only when you're awake, but also when you're sleeping. Remember to start your dream journal and start recording the messages sent to you in your dreams, even if you're not ready to start dabbling in the world of lucid dreaming yet.

As you're hopefully starting to realise, there's so much guidance available to you, and it's so limitless that it doesn't have a bedtime like you do. It's always there, just trying to get through - *will you let it in?*

PART IV CHAPTER 7

PSYCHIC ATTACKS AND PROTECTION

So we've just gone pretty deep into the world beyond the physical, and hopefully you're feeling more than a little excited about exploring your gifts and senses.

But when stepping into this realm you might sometimes feel like you've gotta loosely put your seatbelt on, just in case. I hope you see by now that you don't need to be constantly worried about being possessed or cursed for tapping into your psychic abilities, but one real possibility is receiving negative energy or being part of a psychic attack *(not as scary as it sounds, promise)*.

You might be experiencing a psychic attack if you suddenly:

- ✧ Feel highly anxious or depressed with no noticeable trigger
- ✧ Feel physically sick or uncomfortable with no logical reason as to why you might feel this way
- ✧ Feel fatigued and drained
- ✧ Enter a stage or paralysis, emotional or mental

So what is a psychic attack and how can you protect yourself from this not-so-nice phenomenon?

A psychic attack is when intentionally or unintentionally, negative energy or emotion is sent your way. This could be someone's anger, jealousy, resentment towards you or it could be a conscious intention for bad things to happen to you. It could also come from the living, or the spirit world. Either way, it can affect you mentally, physically and emotionally, *if* you don't know how to handle it.

Every person, empath or not, is vulnerable to these attacks so please don't let this convince you that being an empath or a psychic is a dangerous thing. Us empaths are just a little more susceptible to them, which can actually be a good thing because we're more aware of them, and with awareness comes the ability to prevent them.

Before we cover some tried and tested ways to protect yourself from such attacks, it's important to remember that you hold all the power here. The techniques that we're about to go through can definitely help, but ultimately you are in charge of who accesses your energy and affects your emotions. The more you remind yourself of this fact, the less at risk of these attacks you'll become, and the more safe and powerful you'll feel.

**Technique 1 -
Close Yourself Off**

The last psychic medium I visited used an analogy of mediums being like light bulbs that the spirit world can see when we're asking for messages from them. She said that each night, she thanks the spirit world for their guidance and information and firmly says *'I'm closing off now'* and imagines a lightbulb above her head being switched off. She also does this when she can sense some unfavourable energies trying to enter her energy field.

This is a great way to make yourself less susceptible to psychic attacks as it's a way of saying *'I'm closed!'* to the spirit world. This visualisation can also help to close your own mind off from being so awake.

Energy Practitioner Jill Leigh uses a similar technique. She says that for energy infiltration to take place, you've got to have a drawbridge down, so close the drawbridge and you'll be protected!

Whatever resonates the most should be your chosen option, and it doesn't need to be one of these examples, it could be something totally different. Choose a way to close yourself off and practise it with the knowing that once you're *'closed'*, you're shielded from bad energies.

Technique 2 -
Protection Mantras:

Protection mantras will also help you to strengthen your defences. To make them the most effective, firstly ground yourself and focus by sitting or lying comfortably and taking some deep breaths. Close your eyes if you can. Feel your body or your feet planting into the ground as you allow yourself to feel secure and grounded.

Then choose mantras that resonate with you and make you feel safe.

Some of my favourites are:

- ✧ *'I am divinely protected and therefore I am safe'*
- ✧ *'I hold all the power and that power cannot be taken from me'*
- ✧ *'I am protected from undesirable energy transfer'*
- ✧ *'I am surrounded by a shield of divine protection, nothing can break that'*
- ✧ *'I am protected and grounded at all times and no negative energy can change that'*
- ✧ *'I release all attachments to negativity and only allow love and light to enter my energy field'*

I like to hold my heart or stomach when saying my mantras, or wherever I'm feeling any transferred energy *(anxiety in my stomach for example)*.

Whatever words you feel most comforted by when speaking them will be the right ones for you.

Your subconscious mind doesn't know the difference between reality and fantasy when it comes to what you say, so the more you repeat your mantra, the quicker your subconscious will believe it and you'll feel more safe and protected.

Technique 3 -
Strengthen your Aura

We all have an auric field. It's the electromagnetic field that surrounds us and at its strongest it can measure up to six feet around us! When it's strong it also filters out negative energy and helps us to be in our happiest vibrational state. But when it's weak we're more susceptible to unfavourable energies and are likely to feel lower.

Because we hold all the power, there are a lot of ways we can strengthen our own aura. Below are some tried and tested methods.

- *Pranayama*

Pranayama is a yogic practice that involves the control of the breath. Slowed, conscious breathing is thought to not only improve health but even prolong life, so it's no wonder that it can also have a strengthening effect on our auras. Auras are strongest at their highest vibration, which is when we're at our happiest and healthiest. If we're breathing erratically, as we often do without even realising it, our health and aura strength is bound to be affected.

Our ancestors knew the power of breathwork many years ago, but in more recent times research is beginning to back up what some have previously dismissed as *'woo woo'*. A 2018 Frontiers in Human Neuroscience study reported that slow, mindful breathing *(10 breaths per minute or less)* could increase alertness and comfort and decrease confusion, anxiety and a whole host of other unfavourable emotions. Other research suggests that conscious breathwork can help with energy levels, body temperature and more. Needless to say, breath is a hugely underestimated tool for healing and emotional and spiritual regulation and protection.

Here are some Pranayamas to try:

⟡ ***Sama Vritti Pranayama (Box Breathing)***

Step 1 - Sit comfortably on a chair with your feet on the ground and back straight but relaxed. Close your eyes if you can.

Step 2 - Take a deep breath in for 4 seconds, feeling the walls of your stomach expanding - trying to not breathe only through your chest.

Step 3 - Hold your breath for 4 seconds.

Step 4 - Release your breath for 4 seconds

Repeat this cycle for 4 minutes.

✧ *Nadi Shodhana Pranayama (uses one nostril breathing)*

Step 1 - Sit comfortably and make Vishnu Mudra with your right hand *(holding the index and middle fingers on this hand closed with your thumb)*.

Step 2 - Place the thumb of your right hand on your right nostril, closing it. Inhale through your left nostril.

Step 3 - Before you release the breath, close the left nostril using your right extended fingers as you open the right nostril and exhale through the right nostril.

Step 4 - Repeat on the other side to complete one cycle. Perform these cycles up to five times before returning to slow, dual nostril breathing.

There are so many amazing breathing techniques that can be used to boost your energy and bring you calmness and clarity, these are some great ones to start with. As an empath it will never be a waste of your time just sitting and breathing, as I have no doubt it'll bring you peace and help you to cleanse and reset your energy.

Remember that an aura is an energy field, so the more regularly you can return to conscious, calming and re-energizing breathing habits, the stronger you're keeping your aura, and the more protected you are from bad energies.

Technique 4 -
Have regular time away from artificial electromagnetic fields

It's true, technology is taking over. And I'm not talking about man-eating robots and Artificial Intelligence warlords *(at least not yet..)*, but these days most of us have fallen into the trap of the screens. And it's become normal for it to take 10-15+ hours a day to escape. So normal in fact, that we've forgotten just how unnatural and unhealthy it really is, not just for our bodies, but for our souls, too.

As empaths who are highly sensitive to energetic frequencies, the abundance of technology around us is yet another culprit causing our overwhelming amount of absorbed energy. Our phones, laptops, TVs and other overused devices all give off an electromagnetic field and artificial light, both of which can be draining for anyone, let alone an empath. Not only that, but the content on those devices can also cause huge energy shifts. Whether it's an email from your boss, negativity on social media or depressing news on the TV, observing it through the screen doesn't protect you from the negative impact on your energy, and the regular exposure can be seriously damaging.

Making the conscious effort to have time away from not only this artificial energy, but also the soul-sucking content on our electronic devices, is one of the best ways to stay connected with ourselves, remain grounded and at peace, and keep our energy high and aura strong.

Try scheduling in some *'no tech'* time every day if you can, and that means phone in a different room, tv off at the plug etc.. Take the time to recharge your energy field through a combination of breaks from toxic electricity, breathwork and grounding, and I have no doubt you'll notice a refreshing boost of natural energy and will be more protected from any negative energy trying to let itself in.

Technique 5
Cord Cutting

Imagine a cord between yourself and the person who's bringing you negative energy, or who you're concerned has performed a psychic attack on you *(living or passed over)*. Picture yourself cutting the chord, and consciously release the connection between you both. You could repeat some mantras when doing this, like *'I am releasing this energetic attachment as I only wish to remain attached to positive energies and those who have my best interest at heart'.*

This is a great technique for helping with unhealthy emotional attachment with an ex partner or someone in your life who you know isn't good for you, but you struggle to let them go. It's also great for psychic attacks and the more clearly you can envisage the separation of you and the other person, the faster you'll feel the energetic shift and your power returning back to you.

Technique 6
Have an energetic clear out

Using sage, clear out your environment, ridding it of the negative energy that's tried to impose on your energetic boundaries. Burn White Sage and move it around your body, then around your environment as you consciously remove the negativity from your energy field.

If you suffer with night terrors or tend to experience psychic attacks at night time, burn the sage around all corners of your bed, envisioning the light and good energy replacing the bad. Keep your windows open as you push all the badness out. As you're doing this, picture your space filling up with love, light and positivity, and consciously state that any dark energies are now to leave.

PART IV SUMMARY

Congratulations! You've just opened the door to boundless possibilities of self development and growth in the realm beyond the physical. You now have the tools to unlock your hidden powers as you tap into your sixth sense and psychic abilities in your waking life, and in your sleep.

You've also been provided with some effective protection techniques to keep your energy field strong and you safe. Once you've mastered these all that's left to do is continue exploring your gifts and senses. There's so much guidance and connection just waiting for you, and now you can welcome it all in, safely!

From chatting to the passed over, to using your intuition to predict upcoming events and other people's intentions, and receiving direction and comfort from your guides, you now have a ton of exciting avenues to explore and enjoy.

The key to maximising your gifts is to never forget that you hold all the power, as much as your 3D reality will try to knock your confidence.

You are gifted, your potential to enhance your gifts is limitless, and you have six senses and a whole world beyond what most experience to explore. So don't waste a second debating whether to jump in and start exploring. The worst that could happen is that you decide that the enhanced abilities aren't for you, and you can return to your normal state of being.

I have a sneaky feeling that the world beyond the *'normal'*, will be too magical to leave once you enter though, so I say it's time to lean into that magic and start reaping the rewards.

PART V
USING YOUR EMPATH POWERS TO WORK WITH THE UNIVERSE

PART V CHAPTER 1

MANIFESTATION & WORKING WITH THE UNIVERSE

Our ability to feel so deeply makes us empaths master manifestors. So we can't finish this book without delving into the life changing skill of manifestation.

The beauty of manifestation means that we can create our reality. And don't worry, I haven't been warming you up this whole time to go full *'woo-woo'* on you, this is real stuff! Manifestation might sound unrealistic, but you've actually already manifested your whole life up to this point.

Whether you realise it or not, where you are right now is a direct result of your actions, energy, and perception of yourself and your reality. So to manifest a new, improved reality, you just have to simply align your energy and intentions with the energy of your new desires, and act and *feel* as if you already have what you want. And one of the great things about us empaths? *We feel alright!*

Not only that, but when we're in tune with our gifts, we can shift our energy to match the emotions we choose. Doing this will help us to feel like we already have what we're dreaming of before we physically have it - which is the exact key to manifesting it.

So how do you effectively manifest your desires?

Step 1)
Get really clear on what you really want

This part is super important. If you're wanting to bring your dream house, improved finances, or something else to life, you have to get really clear on that thing. If you're seeking better finances, what is the exact amount you want to see in your bank account? If you want your dream house, what exactly does that look like? Get specific so that the divine can provide. You wouldn't go to a new place without having a specific location in mind, so whatever you're seeking should be no different.

Step 2)
Visualise

Use all of your senses to paint a clear picture of what you're really desiring and imagine living in the reality where you have it. For example, picture yourself walking through your dream house, *what does it look like? In every room? What does it smell like? How do you feel when you're walking through it? Is it warm or is there a breeze?*

If you're seeking better finances, *what is the exact amount you want to see in your bank account? How do you feel when you look at your bank statement? Where are you when you're checking your bank balance, and who's there with you? What are you wearing?*

The key is to be super specific as you're having this imagined experience, allowing yourself to feel the emotions of joy, excitement, comfort, or whatever else having these things will make you feel. Use all six senses to vividly feel into the reality you're desiring. The more regularly you can envisage yourself having the experience, the faster it will become your reality, as you'll be helping your subconscious mind feel safe and familiar having whatever you're desiring.

Step 3)
Tap into the Divine Frequency

Spiritual Mentor Sydney Smith suggests that connecting with your divine frequency can change your manifestation game. This frequency is the energetic level we vibrate at when we're living as our happiest self. When we're at this frequency it's much easier for our manifestations to come in as we're not resisting through stress, anxiety or 'but's and 'how's.

By being in this frequency you can attract everything that's best for you because you're an energetic match for positive things, and you're open and not resistant to receiving.

So how do you tune into this frequency? You do what makes your soul happy.

Think about the times you've been completely at ease, full of joy, peace or happiness. The times you've felt so carefree and optimistic about life. What were you doing in those moments? Laughing with a certain friend? Walking on the beach? Taking yourself on a coffee date? Find time to do those things that make you feel good and you'll naturally connect to your divine frequency.

We're all busy these days, but finding even a small amount of regular time to connect to this and open up space for your manifestations to come in can be life changing. Not only life changing, but also just as, if not more important than doing some of the *'logical'* tasks on our to-do lists. When we're busy *'being productive'*, it's easy to lose sight of what we really want in life. These moments to truly enjoy life are really what we should prioritise, especially as empaths who could always do with this recharge of energy and positivity.

So from now on, try to find some time to do what makes your soul happy. Do something for no logical reason at all other than to make you feel good. Set an intention of what you want to manifest through visualising it, then before you have your *'you'* time, let it out of your mind to prevent any resistance. Don't think about how it will manifest, just stay connected to the divine frequency and watch how your manifestation comes in.. Because it will.

Step 4)
Switching to an Abundant Mindset vs a Victim Mindset

It's pretty common for us empaths to see our gifts as more of a curse. I hope by this point you're seeing that's not the case. But if you don't yet, there's another benefit of not seeing yourself as hindered by your gifts, and that's that people who see themselves as lucky, abundant or gifted, will attract and manifest so much more goodness to them than those who feel hindered.

This is because if we don't believe that we can have, do or be something, we're right. If we believe that as an empath, we're too sensitive to handle the pressure that might come with the new position we're dreaming of, we'll subconsciously sabotage getting that new position. It's human nature to want to protect ourselves, which is why it's super important to practise everything taught throughout this book to get in tune with your gifts, and to see yourself as gifted and abundant vs burdened and fragile.

Switching to this mindset of expecting good things to happen to you will have you super-attracting the good!

Taking these steps can be nothing short of life changing. Remember to prioritise your energy protection too, so that you can effectively manifest and bring your wildest dreams to life.

As well as taking these steps to manifest your dream life, here are some tried and tested techniques to help you become a master manifestor.

Manifestation Techniques

✧ **The 777 Method**

This is a simple technique that gets you regularly and consistently thinking about what you want to manifest, and it can lead to results in just a week *(or less!)*

All you've got to do is write down what you're desiring seven times in the morning, and seven times in the evening, for seven consecutive days. The key with any manifestation technique is to write as though you already have your desire.

For example:

> *'I'm so happy to be making an extra $500 a month!'*

Writing as if you already have it puts you in the energy of gratitude rather than longing, and if your subconscious is being told you have something, it will find ways to make your reality match that belief.

In numerology, 777 is associated with the fulfilment of dreams and good luck, adding to the power of this technique.

✧ *Scripting*

Scripting is like physical visualisation as it's just you writing about your desires as you're vividly picturing living in them. The key with this method again is to write in the present or past tense, as if you're experiencing your wish fulfilment.

As empaths we tend to have creative and emotional minds, so use this to your advantage when doing this technique. Allow yourself to get into the flow with your writing, and free write until you're feeling excited and grateful for the life you're manifesting.

For example:

> *'I had another amazing day at my new job today. I'm so happy that I've gained this new position and it feels so good to be receiving a much bigger salary. I feel so much more fulfilled in what I do and I'm so grateful to be living my dream life so soon!'*

Even if none of these things have actually manifested yet, write as if they have. The more you immerse yourself in this vision, the sooner it will become your reality.

Some master manifestors do Scripting at night and put their paper under their pillow. This way your dream vision is vivid in your mind when you're at your most relaxed, and your brain could well find solutions to get you to that dream life whilst you're sleeping.

✧ Manifesting With Water

Water is an amazing medium to use to help with manifestation. If you want to manifest feeling a certain way, perhaps to help you tap into your Divine Frequency, or to just feel more uplifted, you can use it to shift your energy very quickly.

Fill up a glass of clean, fresh water, and speak positive words as you hold onto the glass. Picture light and love actually going into the water as you channel your energy into it.

Some great phrases to use are:

- ✧ *'When I drink this water, I will be filled with love and happiness'*
- ✧ *'This pure water will cleanse me of negative energy'*
- ✧ *'I am grateful for this water, as it will refresh me with positivity'*

Once you've spent around 30 seconds visualising this water building up the energy you're seeking, drink it and say thank you. This is one of the easiest and most effective ways to manifest an energy shift and the key is to really visualise the benefits you'll get once you've consumed the water.

This may sound like woo-woo, but many studies have been done on the effects on water when positive vs negative words are spoken to it. For example, it's pretty impressive to see the difference in ice formation patterns when warm words of affirmation have been spoken to it, vs words of anger and hate. *Try it out for yourself and I have no doubt you'll feel the positive shifts!*

Extra Tips For Manifesting As An Empath

So you've now got some effective techniques to help you with manifesting all you desire. These techniques can be used by anyone to create their dream life, no matter how different your current reality might look *(yes, really!)*. But how can you harness your empath gifts to truly maximise your manifesting powers?

Tip 1) Address your *'receiving wound'*

Us empaths love to give. But in order to manifest our desires, we must learn to receive, too. The universe can't provide what we're asking for if we're not open to actually receiving it. So start by learning to receive whenever you can, whether it be a compliment, a gesture from another person, or someone buying you something. Rather than feeling guilty or unworthy, learning to gratefully receive these little things will help you to welcome in bigger blessings.

Vocally telling the universe you're ready to receive will also help. Some mantras you could use are:

- ❖ *I am worthy of receiving good things*
- ❖ *It is safe for me to receive my biggest blessings*
- ❖ *I am a giver therefore I deserve to receive*

Picturing whatever you're desiring coming towards you without resistance as you say these mantras can help them to manifest too.

Tip 2) Realise your magic

I hope by now you're seeing just how much power and magic you hold as an empath. You have strong senses *(all six!)*, and abilities that most people will never even tap into. And developing the genuine belief that you are special and gifted, can seriously help you to manifest. Think about it, if you believe you're not gifted, special, or lucky, you'll likely begin to expect bad luck and a series of unfortunate events, and that expectation will become your reality. But if you believe you're gifted, good hearted and open to receiving good in your life, good things will inevitably happen for you.

Believing that you have special gifts and are in tune with all six senses, have deepened intuition and are awakened and open, can help you to welcome in opportunities, people and thoughts that can help you to manifest the life of your dreams. So whenever you're doubting how special you are, remind yourself of your best empath qualities and your magic and power - because those traits are magnets for your biggest manifestations.

Tip 3) Bypass your sensitivity *(in some situations)*

As a highly sensitive empath, sensitivity is present in most situations in our lives. And while sensitivity is a superpower, sometimes it can be a pesky manifestation hinderer. This is because when we're waiting for our manifestations to come in, life around us doesn't stop. Bad things can still happen and when we're easily affected by those things, it can be hard to trust that good things are still on their way, and not just accept that the bad is more prevalent and likely to stay.

For example, let's say you're working towards a huge financial goal, and random costs keep popping up that feel like they're blocking your manifestation. It would be easy to become emotionally affected and buy into the belief that your manifestation just isn't happening for you. But by doing that you're hindering what you're wishing for, because you're letting your emotions buy into the reality that you're not getting what you want. This is where you need to bypass your sensitivity and naturally triggered negative emotions, and try to believe that you're undoubtedly getting what you desire, no matter how unrealistic it might currently seem.

As previously taught, you should absolutely acknowledge any emotions that crop up, but then release them through your preferred method. Remind yourself that if you've never experienced what you're manifesting before *(like riches, an amazing job, a loving partner)*, then of course emotions like fear, anxiety and stress will arise, because your subconscious mind will be trying to keep you safe from the unknown. So as you're releasing these emotions through deep breaths or whatever way works best, affirm that it's safe to step into this new reality. With time and repetition, your subconscious will believe you, and any fears and resistance will ease.

Mastering the art of delusion is possibly the best hack to manifesting your biggest dreams. It might seem silly to convince yourself that you're getting these big blessings when everything *(and maybe everyone)*, in your reality seems to be suggesting otherwise, but by tuning into your power and trusting in the unseen, you can, and will, achieve whatever you're desiring.

Don't let sensitivity, doubts or negative emotions try to convince you that you're not getting what you've asked for. The universe is always listening and waiting to provide. So just ask and trust, and you will receive.

PART V CHAPTER 2

CRYSTALS

We can't talk about working with the universe without mentioning one of the best natural resources it provides - Crystals.

Crystals have been used for thousands of years for their healing, protection and numerous other benefits, and they're the perfect companion for us empaths. In this chapter you'll find a list of the most beneficial crystals for you, but first let's get into how to use them, and how to know which ones to pick.

Some of the best ways to use crystals are:

✧ Holding a crystal during your meditation routine to amplify the benefits.
✧ Keeping one in your pocket, purse or even in your bra - to carry its benefits with you wherever you go.
✧ Putting them on or in your bath.

⋄ Placing one next to your bed, or simply holding it in your hand as you fall asleep.

How do you know which crystals are right for you?

In this chapter you'll find some of the crystals that are well known for being beneficial for empaths, and some that have helped me personally. But besides from what little old me recommends, how do you know which crystals you should actually use?

Your sixth sense. Remember when I said it's always there, just waiting to guide you? Well when choosing crystals is a perfect time to let its guidance come through. If you're standing in front of a table of different crystals, you'll naturally be drawn to one, or a few. This happens to me every time, and now that I've learned to trust my intuition more, I'll often close my eyes and let my senses guide me to the crystal I need without letting the aesthetics of each crystal confuse my judgement. *Try it!*

Because crystals all have different properties, we can benefit from all of them at different points. When you're looking for a new crystal, ask yourself what you're seeking at that point in your life. Do you want to feel more at peace? Are you wanting to feel more protected from negative energy? Or something else? Whatever you're seeking there's a crystal out there to help you, so let your intuition guide you to the right one. Of course crystals aren't a replacement for the deeper inner work and protection techniques that we've already covered, but they're a great addition.

Here are some of the most beneficial crystals for us empaths:

✧ *Clear Quartz*

This crystal is well known for symbolising spiritual growth and healing. It's a personal favourite of mine and I was incredibly drawn towards it after going through a bad break up, when I had no idea about the meaning of crystals. In my experience, it can bring you a nice feeling of peace and comfort, and it's renowned for bringing balance, love and positivity.

✧ *Black Tourmaline*

This crystal is arguably the most well known crystal when it comes to protection. It's known to protect against negative energies, psychic attacks and any other nasties trying to creep into your energy field - so there's no wonder it's one of the best crystals for us empaths.

Placing some black tourmaline by your front door or on your window sills is a great way to keep your home a positive energy zone. If you work with energy vampires or generally negative characters, keeping some on your desk can help to protect you too.

✧ *Obsidian*

This is another crystal renowned for protecting against negative energy. It soaks up the energy, so that you don't have to hold it all *(which means it does need to be cleansed often)*.

Because of the way this crystal absorbs the energy, it's great for keeping with you in negative environments to capture the energy, then releasing the negativity by cleansing it under clean running water, visualising the bad energy running out of it and down the drain. If you have Obsidian with you when you're in an overwhelming environment and you start to feel yourself getting flustered, picture all of the chaotic energy going into the crystal. Then cleanse it as soon as you can to release the overwhelm.

✧ Amethyst

This is one of the most well-known crystals and there's no wonder with how beautiful it is. Not only is it aesthetically pleasing, but it also has calming properties that are rumoured to help with feelings of anxiety, negative vibrations, and emotional overwhelm *(sounds like it was made for an empath, right?)*. Mystics in the old ages even used this crystal to help with everything from spider bites and acne, to raising consciousness - there's no debating that this is one of the *'must-have'* crystals, whether you're an empath or not!

Try placing an Amethyst crystal under your bed before you sleep to help with nightmares, or carry it with you for spiritual and emotional protection wherever you go.

✧ Tree Agate

Our final crystal is Tree Agate, and it's known for its stabilising and grounding properties. For us empaths who can struggle with overwhelm, holding onto this crystal can help us gain balance and feelings of security and stability. Try holding this crystal when you're doing your grounding or energy protection practises to enhance the effects.

There are so many other crystals out there that I have no doubt you'll benefit from. But to save any overwhelm *(us empaths defi-*

nitely don't need any more of that!), I'd suggest trying some of these first, or picking any others that you intuitively feel drawn to.

Before we close this chapter, it's important to know how to cleanse and recharge your crystals, afterall, they're just energy that's dense enough to have formed matter.. Like us, really! And just like us, we don't want them holding onto negative energy, so we should regularly rid them of any nastiness.

Tips to cleanse and recharge your crystals

1) Place Under Sunlight Or Moonlight

The sun and moon have different energies, which I'm sure as an empath you know innately. Placing your crystals under the bright sun or a full moon is a great way to recharge them.

Under the sun they can be charged with vibrancy and vitality, and under the full moon they can be blessed with strong feminine energy and deeply cleansed. The moon has many different phases that offer different benefits to your crystals, so it's worth looking into those once you're more familiar with using crystals. It's also important to mention that not every crystal does well under the bright sun, so do your research before you place any outside to recharge.

2) Bury Them

It's no secret that the earth beneath us has some seriously impressive healing and energetic benefits, it's why grounding works so well. It makes sense then, that our crystals can benefit from the ground's electrical charge by being buried in it. Bury your crystals overnight or for 24 hours and when you dig them up again they should be cleansed and full of energy again *(just don't forget where you buried them, like I have an embarrassing number of times!)*.

3) Place In Salt Water

We know that bathing in salt water can have lots of positive effects on the human body, so it's no surprise that it can also benefit our crystals. If you live near a beach, collect some fresh saltwater and put it in a glass with your crystals in and allow them to cleanse and recharge. If you don't live near a beach, use some clean water and Himilayan rock salt to get the same benefits.

So there you have it, you now have another handy tool in your toolbox to protect you against negative energy and help you to stay grounded. I can't wait for you to feel the benefits that crystals can bring to your life. Remember to use your sixth sense to pick out the most beneficial ones for you, and keep them *(and yourself)* charged up and ready to fight off the nasties all around you.

PART V SUMMARY

Your openness as an empath makes it easier for you to work with the Divine/Universe/Source and improve your life in many ways. Through manifestation techniques, crystals and other gifts from the Universe, you can enhance your powers and gain comfort and reassurance along your path.

I hope this part of the guide has made you feel even more excited about your gifts and how you can use them to improve your life. Remember to never forget the infinite power that's available to you and just how much you can achieve with your mind and a little help from the Universe.

CONCLUSION

Congratulations, you made it! I hope you now see that being an empath is truly a gift. It allows us to experience the highest highs with no filter. It allows us to be more connected to those we love and those we don't yet know. We can communicate with our energy and warmth, and that alone will allow us to make so many beautiful connections in this lifetime that others might never be lucky enough to welcome in.

We also have a headstart when it comes to developing real life superpowers, and I hope this guide has helped to demystify the psychic world and make it much less spooky. We each have magic inside of us that can be used to manifest our deepest desires, enhance our intuition, and communicate with the unseen; it's a gift that most people will never know exists, but it will continue to enrich our lives the more we explore it.

It's my deep hope that you now feel more equipped to face the world with a new sense of empowerment and confidence, ready to protect yourself from negative energy that isn't yours to carry, and ready to allow your sixth sense to guide you through the rollercoaster ride that is life as an empath.

This guide has provided all the tips you'll need to feel safe in and empowered by your gifts, and I can't wait for you to become the most grounded, confident and powerful version of yourself possible when you apply them.

Please always remember that you deserve to put yourself first and protect your precious energy, because at your highest frequency you're a true natural healer who radiates love and light, and who can manifest a reality that most will never know is possible.

You're a gifted empath and you are powerful and limitless. I hope you never forget it!

From one gifted empath to another, I wish you peace, positivity, and power - no matter how bumpy this ride might get. I lovingly thank you for coming on this journey with me and for sharing your time and precious energy. It's time to go out there and spread your powerful magic ~ there's a whole world out there just waiting to be blessed by your gifts.

THERE'S A GIFT FOR YOU ON THE NEXT PAGE!

But first.. I want to offer you the chance to spread some of your magic.. In the form of guiding other empaths to this book.

By leaving a review on Amazon, you'll help this book become more visible to those who need it, potentially greatly helping other empaths on their journey.

Also, as an independent author, every single review goes a really long way, so I thank you in advance for not only helping my dreams come true, but for helping me to help others.

Leaving a review is free and shouldn't take more than 60 seconds! Just go back to this book on Amazon to leave your rating/review.

Ok ok.. Enough of helping me and others, it's time to take some goodness for yourself *(as I so passionately encourage!)*. Read on for your present.

A SMALL GIFT, JUST FOR YOU

I wanted to finish this book off by giving you a little gift if you made it to the end, and I have no doubt that the next few pages will help you on your journey, so from me to you, enjoy!

Affirmations for Empaths

Learning to appreciate your empath gifts takes time. It's not a case of someone *(like me)* telling you that you're strong, gifted, etc.. and you wholeheartedly believing it and never struggling with your heavy emotions ever again. There will be hurdles along your journey of finding comfort as an empath, situations will test you and make you doubt your strength, or your confidence, so it's important to regularly remind yourself, and teach your subconscious, that your empath gifts are benefits. Affirmations are a great way to do this. Some people find it silly at first to say affirmations out loud, but a lot of great leaders and most successful, whole, healed people have used affirmations to get them where they are mentally, socially and professionally.

So try to surpass feeling uncomfortable, and say affirmations out loud until you're at the stage of being in agreement and alignment with the words coming out of your mouth. Even if you don't initially believe what you're saying to be true about yourself, repeat it until you do, because the phrases will become ingrained in your subconscious until your conscious mind believes them.

Here are some affirmations to get you started - these are specifically aimed at the empath in you.

- ⟡ I am a natural healer
- ⟡ I can use my energy to help others
- ⟡ I care - and that's a benefit not a burden
- ⟡ I am compassionate
- ⟡ My sensitivity enables me to truly live
- ⟡ I am strong
- ⟡ I am kind
- ⟡ I am real
- ⟡ My ability to feel deeply is a gift
- ⟡ I trust my intuition
- ⟡ I can positively impact the lives of others without sacrificing my own
- ⟡ I can succeed without compromising my character
- ⟡ I can achieve anything I set my mind to
- ⟡ I can motivate others with my positive energy
- ⟡ It is not my responsibility to make others happy
- ⟡ My happiness comes first
- ⟡ It is not selfish to put myself first
- ⟡ My emotional nature makes me passionate - it is a gift
- ⟡ To be sensitive does not make me weak

Activity: It may feel uncomfortable, awkward, or unlike you, but your final activity is to start saying your affirmations right now. Pick one or as many as you like and say them outloud in the mirror. Pick ones that even if you don't believe right now, you really want to believe one day. This will be the start of truly believing in yourself and ingraining a confident, resilient attitude despite the ups and downs that come with being an empath.

JOIN THEMAGICWITHIN FAMILY!

If you'd like to connect with a community of like-minded, caring souls, come and join our MagicWithin family on social media!

*You can find us on **Instagram at @TheMagicWithin_**
Or come hang out in our **private Facebook group: TheMagicWithin***

*And if you'd like more regular tips on everything from harnessing your empath traits and sensitivity, to improving confidence and clarity in all areas of your life, you can join our email list by emailing us here: **samaria@themagicwithin.world** (we won't send you a load of spammy rubbish, promise!)*

REFERENCES

1. Taylor, R. (2020, September 23). Jim Carrey Commencement Speech Transcript 2014 at Maharishi University of Management. *Rev.* https://www.rev.com/blog/transcripts/jim-carrey-commencement-speech-transcript-2014-at-maharishi-university-of-management
2. Murphy, M. (2018, April 15). Neuroscience Explains Why You Need To Write Down Your Goals If You Actually Want To Achieve Them. *Forbes.* https://www.forbes.com/sites/markmurphy/2018/04/15/neuroscience-explains-why-you-need-to-write-down-your-goals-if-you-actually-want-to-achieve-them/?sh=32494d937905
3. Team, B. a. S. (2023, January 5). Why giving is good for your health. *Cleveland Clinic.* https://health.clevelandclinic.org/why-giving-is-good-for-your-health/
4. *Are You an Empath? with Lee Harris.* (n.d.-b). Gaia. https://www.gaia.com/video/are-you-empath-lee-harris?fullplayer=feature
5. Robbins, L. (2021, September 13). *Energetic Boundaries: 5 boundary setting Tricks - Wild Tree Psychotherapy.* Wild Tree Psychotherapy. https://wildtreewellness.com/energetic-boundaries/
6. Rugnetta, M. (2023, July 28). *Neuroplasticity | Different Types, Facts, & research.* Encyclopedia Britannica. https://www.britannica.com/science/neuroplasticity
7. Stokes, V. (2023, February 14). *Intuitive empaths: signs, types, downsides, and Self-Care.* Healthline. https://www.healthline.com/health/intuitive-empaths#the-science
8. *Invisible acts of power.* (n.d.). Gaia. https://www.gaia.com/video/invisible-acts-power?fullplayer=feature
9. MSc, S. D. R. C. (2023, February 6). *Vitamin D benefits.* Healthline. https://www.healthline.com/health/food-nutrition/benefits-vitamin-d#fights-disease

REFERENCES

10. Granneman, J. (2018). 27 quotes every highly sensitive person will instantly relate to. *Sensitive Refuge.* https://highlysensitiverefuge.com/highly-sensitive-person-quotes/
11. *How to surround yourself with good people in your life | tonyrobbins.com.* (2021, December 30). tonyrobbins.com. https://www.tonyrobbins.com/stories/business-mastery/surround-yourself-with-quality-people/
12. *thriving.* (2023). https://dictionary.cambridge.org/dictionary/english/thriving
13. Eby, D. (2022). Joss Stone On Being An Artist and Empath. *The Creative Mind.* https://thecreativemind.net/1526/joss-stone-artist-and-empath/
14. Smith, S. (2022). 4 Tips to Manifest Your Dreams as an Empath — Adventuring with Poseidon Wellness | Spiritual Mentor. *Adventuring With Poseidon.* https://www.adventuringwithposeidon.com/blog/4-tips-to-manifest-your-dreams-as-an-empath
15. *View of Applications of lucid dreams and their effects on the mood upon awakening.* (n.d.). https://journals.ub.uni-heidelberg.de/index.php/IJoDR/article/view/33114/pdf
16. Noyed, D., & Noyed, D. (2023). 5 ways to get more REM Sleep. *Sleep Foundation.* https://www.sleepfoundation.org/stages-of-sleep/how-to-get-more-rem-sleep
17. *How To Cleanse Crystals: 9 Crucial Practices You Need To Know.* (n.d.). Tiny Rituals. https://tinyrituals.co/blogs/tiny-rituals/how-to-cleanse-crystals
18. *How to use crystals for protection at home.* (2020, April 27). https://www.penguin.co.uk/articles/2019/02/how-to-use-crystals-for-protection-at-home-hausmagick
19. mindbodygreen. (2023, January 13). *6 Crystals To Protect Yourself From Toxic People & Negative Energy.* Mindbodygreen. https://www.mindbodygreen.com/articles/crystals-for-protection
20. *Clear Quartz Meaning: Healing Properties & Uses.* (n.d.). Tiny Rituals. https://tinyrituals.co/blogs/tiny-rituals/clear-quartz-meaning-healing-properties-uses#:

21. Ripoll, M. M. (n.d.). *Crystallography. The structure of crystals. Early historical notes.* https://www.xtal.iqfr.csic.es/Cristalografia/parte_01_1-en.html#:

22. *The College of Psychic Studies: On demand: Mediumship training: What is the difference between psychic mediumship.* (n.d.). The College of Psychic Studies. https://www.collegeofpsychicstudies.co.uk/on-demand/mediumship-training/what-is-the-difference-between-psychic-mediumship/

23. Manifest, B. &. (2022, May 20). *4 Lessons I learned Trying to manifest as an empath - bloom and manifest.* Bloom and Manifest. https://www.bloomandmanifest.com/lessons-trying-to-manifest-as-an-empath/

24. Keithley, Z. (2023). 8 Powerful Manifestation Games To Attract Your Desires. *Zanna Keithley.* https://zannakeithley.com/manifestation-games/

25. Zaccaro, A., Piarulli, A., Laurino, M., Garbella, E., Menicucci, D., Neri, B., & Gemignani, A. (2018). How Breath-Control Can Change Your Life: A systematic review on Psycho-Physiological correlates of slow breathing. *Frontiers in Human Neuroscience, 12.* https://doi.org/10.3389/fnhum.2018.00353

26. Blakeman, E. (2022). The power of '777.' *Kintsugi Space.* https://kintsugispace.com/the-power-of-777/#:

27. Roane, D. (2022). How To Use The 777 Method To Manifest Anything You Want In 7 Days. *YourTango.* https://www.yourtango.com/self/how-use-777-manifestation-technique#:

28. *The College of Psychic Studies: On demand: Mediumship training: What is the difference between psychic mediumship.* (n.d.-b). The College of Psychic Studies. https://www.collegeofpsychicstudies.co.uk/on-demand/mediumship-training/what-is-the-difference-between-psychic-mediumship/

29. Wahbeh, H., Niebauer, E., Delorme, A., Carpenter, L., Radin, D., & Yount, G. (2021). A case study of extended human capacity perception during Energy Medicine treatments using mixed methods analysis. *Explore-the*

Journal of Science and Healing, 17(1), 70–78. https://doi.org/10.1016/j.explore.2020.10.006

30. Torres, N. (2023, March 20). What Does it Mean to Be Creative (+ Real Life Examples). *Imaginated.* https://www.imaginated.com/blog/what-does-it-mean-to-be-creative/
31. *E-Motion.* (n.d.). Gaia. https://www.gaia.com/video/e-motion
32. Jain, R. (2023, July 27). Complete Guide To The 7 Chakras: Symbols, Effects & How To Balance | Arhanta Yoga Blog. *Arhanta Yoga Ashrams.* https://www.arhantayoga.org/blog/7-chakras-introduction-energy-centers-effect/

EMPATH & PSYCHIC ABILITIES

YOUR PRACTICAL GUIDE TO EASING OVERWHELM,
PROTECTING YOUR ENERGY, GAINING CONFIDENCE
IN YOUR GIFTS & DEVELOPING YOUR INTUITIVE
ABILITIES TO UNLOCK YOUR SIXTH SENSE

THEMAGICWITHIN

www.ingramcontent.com/pod-product-compliance
Lightning Source LLC
Chambersburg PA
CBHW071439080526
44587CB00014B/1910